ADVOCACY PRACTICE FOR
SOCIAL JUSTICE

Also Available from Lyceum Books, Inc.

Advocacy Practice for Social Justice

Richard Hoefer
University of Texas
at Arlington

LYCEUM
BOOKS, INC.

Chicago, Illinois

© Lyceum Books, Inc., 2006

Published by

Lyceum Books, Inc.
5758 S. Blackstone Ave.
Chicago, Illinois 60637
773+643-1903 (Fax)
773+643-1902 (Phone)
lyceum@lyceumbooks.com
http://www.lyceumbooks.com

Library of Congress Cataloging-in-Publication Data

Hoefer, Richard.
    Advocacy practice for social justice : incorporating advocacy into the generalist model / Richard Hoefer.
        p. cm.
    Includes bibliographical references and index.
    ISBN 0-925065-93-5
    1. Social advocacy. I. Title.
HV40.H628   2005
361.3—dc22

                                                              2005009034

To my parents, for shaping the past
To Catheleen, for making the present
To Sharon, Kate, and Chris, for creating the future

CONTENTS

PREFACE

My introduction to advocacy came early in life, and the examples came from my father. He did not always have a good idea of the best way to go about his advocacy, but I learned from him that it is important to tell those with decision-making authority what is wrong with the world so that something can be done to fix it. One of my early attempts at advocacy was a spontaneous protest at a high school pep club rally that resulted in me being suspended for several days. It also led, however, to a high level of name recognition and to a successful campaign to become sophomore class president. From that position, I was able to make at least one or two important changes for the better, probably because I then had the reputation of being willing to work at making change happen.

I carried these experiences with me as I planned and wrote this book. But I also had a great deal of additional knowledge that I had acquired over the years. Some of this knowledge was "book learning," gained during my education in social work, political science, and sociology. Some of the knowledge was from serving as a board member and president of T-PACE, the National Association of Social Workers' political action committee in Texas. Some of the knowledge came from leading a neighborhood organization and other activities. I wanted to share the fruits of my study and experience.

Still, there are already good books on advocacy available, and I had to figure out what I could add that would make the effort worthwhile. As I read several books on the subject by my friends and colleagues Mark Ezell, Karen Haynes and Jim Mickelson, Bruce Jansson, Willard Richan, and Robert Schneider and Lori Lester, I found at least two areas where I thought I could bring something fresh, interesting, and useful to the field.

First, previous books tend to talk about the need to describe advocacy apart from the rest of social work and show its distinctiveness.

Sure, every social worker should *do* advocacy, it is argued, but these other books, nonetheless, describe advocacy as a special endeavor that should be examined as a "thing in its own category." I, too, believe that advocacy practice is unique, but only in the same way that all practice modalities are unique—different skills may be needed and different techniques may be used. But what strikes me about advocacy is how much it is similar to all other social work practice approaches.

Advocacy is conceived of in this book as a process designed for problem solving, and, thus, it easily fits into a generalist model of social work. No other book on advocacy lists generalist social work practice in its index, so bringing a problem-solving perspective to the presentation of advocacy practice is a new addition to the field. Interestingly, books on generalist practice, even those on generalist practice in macro-settings, do not apply the larger generalist approach to advocacy. Again, advocacy is seen as part of social work practice, but not in the form of a problem-solving technique. So, this book is laid out in a way that follows a typical problem-solving pattern that should be familiar to almost every social worker in the United States. By showing how similar advocacy is to other types of social work practice, I hope to take away the seemingly foreign nature of advocacy and help make social workers more comfortable in taking on this vital work. I believe that this approach also clearly shows the interconnections between the different theaters of advocacy, such as within the legislative, executive, and judicial branches of government.

The second contribution I hope to make with this book is to show the large amount of empirical research that applies to advocacy. I have had to learn a great deal about topics that are not necessarily first thought of as being related to social work advocacy in order to write this book. The political science literature has been an especially useful source, but so too have other fields, such as psychology, sociology, and business. Compared to the authors of other books that were written half a decade or more ago, I have the advantage of several years of additional research to comb through for insights and evidence. Thus, I establish an "evidence-based" advocacy practice that builds on the practice wisdom that has been the norm for the area. Certainly other authors have used the research available to them, but this book has the most recent information available from a variety of academic disciplines.

Finally, I wanted to put all of this information in a shorter book, one that would be supportive of the strengths of other texts or be able to be read on its own by someone interested in advocacy who did not have the time to read a very long book.

WHO IS THIS BOOK FOR?

Advocacy Practice for Social Justice is designed primarily for students at both BSW and MSW levels and for practicing social workers who need a focused yet comprehensive reference on advocacy. This book is primarily intended for two types of courses. The first type is *introductory or specialized social welfare policy courses*, in which only part of the course is devoted to understanding and conducting advocacy. The rest of the course is an overview of social welfare policy or a deeper look within a particular policy arena, such as mental health or child welfare. The second type is *macropractice courses*, in which more information on advocacy is desired than what is found in the generalist texts currently available.

Other potential audiences include students in elective courses focusing on advocacy (particularly those on a quarter or shortened term calendar) or courses with a service-learning component, where the project assigned requires attempting to influence policy.

THE PLAN OF THE BOOK

As noted above, *Advocacy Practice for Social Justice* is based on the generalist approach to social work practice. As such, I present a step-by-step idealized approach to advocacy, even while admitting that advocacy in real life frequently returns to earlier steps and sometimes skims over other steps rather quickly. Still, I designed the bulk of the book to be used in a front-to-back way.

Chapter 1 introduces advocacy practice as a specialized practice modality within the larger generalist framework. Chapter 1 also introduces four major contextual trends affecting social work practice and shows how the material in the book helps advocates handle them. Students who are thoroughly familiar with the generalist approach to social work practice may find some of this material familiar, but the chapter provides an overview of most of the book so is important to include.

Chapter 2 discusses the reason social workers conduct advocacy—to promote social justice. The ethical imperatives for advocacy, as set forth in the National Association of Social Workers' Code of Ethics, are explored, as are the terms *social justice* and *distributive justice*. With the foundation of why to engage in advocacy laid, the next several chapters explain the steps of the advocacy process one after the next. I provide several examples of situations where ethical conflicts may be present as a critical thinking activity and application of chapter material.

Chapter 3, "Getting Involved," discusses the first step. Going beyond mere exhortation to "be involved," this chapter provides a clear, research-based understanding of why people are involved. It describes a model of involvement and the variables that can be influenced to increase the level of involvement in advocacy. In that sense, then, it is a blueprint for advocacy capacity building. Readers can examine their lives to determine which factors are working in promoting their interest and abilities in advocacy and how they might affect these variables in their own situation.

Chapter 4, "Understanding the Issue," begins with a vignette about one of my real-life situations. I present a five-step process for gaining understanding of an issue. Of special note are several techniques that I present in the chapter to aid decision making, particularly when developing solutions to addressing the issue and in understanding the impact of various solutions on social justice. These are very appropriate for immediate use in a group role-play situation or for individual reflection.

Chapter 5, "Planning in Advocacy," provides information on what planning is, how to conduct it, and how to know when it is time to move to action. A planning tool, called an advocacy map, is introduced as an aid to the planning process. An offshoot of the logic model concept often used in program planning, the advocacy map assists advocates in keeping the big picture goals in mind even while planning the details of who will do what and why, when taking action. I provide two examples of advocacy maps, and readers can use the blank template in thinking about their own advocacy projects.

Chapter 6 presents information on negotiation and persuasion. Using the latest research on these topics, I present readers with a comprehensive way to plan their pitch, from how to frame an issue to understanding the mind-set of the target of advocacy and what works to change it. This material can quickly be used by readers in everyday situations at home and at work as well as within an advocacy context.

In chapter 7, "Presenting Your Information Effectively," I also rely on recent scholarship to assist readers in showcasing what they have to say in the most effective way. The information in this chapter links with the previous chapter in order to allow readers to see the full range of options available to get the word out to indirect targets as well as the direct targets of an advocacy effort.

Evaluation of advocacy efforts is the topic of chapter 8. I return to the advocacy maps introduced in chapter 5 to show how this planning tool is extremely useful in evaluation. In addition to the usual aspects of evaluation, such as process and outcome evaluation, I also introduce the idea of "context monitoring," which is used to keep abreast of how an organization is perceived by others in the policy arena. Context monitoring is an essential, though frequently overlooked, element of an advocacy group's effectiveness.

After an advocacy project is completed and evaluated, the tendency is to pack up one's bags and move on to the next campaign or issue. The purpose of chapter 9 is to squash this tendency. Monitoring the regulation-writing process and implementing a policy are important to creating and maintaining social justice. I include specific recommendations for how to be an effective advocate in each part of this phase of the advocacy process.

Chapter 10, "Integrating Advocacy into Your Social Work Practice," presents a brief history of advocacy in social work and the lessons learned throughout the book. I could have presented this material earlier in the book to provide the historical context of advocacy in social work for readers, and, in fact, some may want to read this chapter before the chapters on the advocacy process. I have put it at the end because many students have told me that they have a much greater positive regard for the history of social work advocacy *after* they have tried to do it. Too often, historical overviews are seen as nonessential fluff by readers who want to get to the "meat" of the topic. It is often only when students have tried to emulate the pioneers of advocacy, and seen the difficulties and barriers that can block the way, that students can truly appreciate what others have done. By leaving this material until the end, I hope the inspiration of others' actions is blended with the lessons learned in today's environment.

ACKNOWLEDGMENTS

The writing of a book requires a substantial investment of time and energy, thought and learning, writing and revision. Without an array of understanding people surrounding me, this manuscript would never have been completed. I want to thank David Follmer, for allowing me the time to finish, and those who helped critique the completed draft. These ideas have been tested out on scores of students at the University of Texas at Arlington, and those students deserve extra credit for helping me understand better ways to present specific material. Their questions have helped me form answers.

—Richard Hoefer

Chapter 1

THE GENERALIST MODEL AND ADVOCACY PRACTICE

Ms. Jones enters your office, head hanging down, two young children at her side. After she sits down, you ask her how you can be of help to her today. "Nobody can do anything for me today," she exclaims. "The air conditioning is out in my apartment building, and the weather forecast is for highs over 100 degrees for the rest of the week. This is the third time this summer that the air has broken down, and the landlord sure is no good. He just wants the rent paid on time. It's bad for my kids' health—Michael here's got asthma. My neighbors and I are sure fed up with this nonsense! But there's nothing we can do."

Social workers are called upon to assist people in need. Needs can be physical, mental, social, or societal, and social workers must be able to provide help for all types of needs. People come with problems, hoping that social workers will be able to assist them in resolving their issues. Social work education prepares social workers with a set of knowledge and skills that will enable them to help clients. Situations that social workers face in their professional life certainly include problems that bedevil individuals and families. But one of the defining elements of social work practice is that social workers are trained to see the connections between problems that affect individuals and problems that affect larger numbers of people because of organizational or governmental policies that impose costs, monetary and otherwise, on or deny services to people in need.

Examples of the types of costs that people in need must pay as a result of organizational or governmental policies include spending time waiting in a first-come, first-served line to apply for financial assistance;

paying higher prices at local markets in low-income areas because public transportation is not available to other shopping areas; paying high fees to cash checks because banks are not located nearby; and having higher levels of cancer and other diseases because low-income housing is located near industrial dumping zones or other sources of considerable pollution.

Often people in need are denied services because organizations and governments change the definition of eligibility (e.g., a person with a savings account with more than $500, rather than the former maximum of $1,000, is no longer eligible for a program). Service is also denied when income eligibility levels are shifted downward, leading to more people not qualifying because they earn too much, and when the benefits available are restricted, for example, when an organization does not pay for mental health services.

Besides linking the micro scale of individuals to the macro scale of organizations, communities, and larger entities, social workers have in many cases adopted a concept known as "generalist social work practice." Although there are many different approaches to generalist social work practice, all agree that this practice is a "problem-solving" method (Perlman, 1957). This method, according to its proponents, can be used to address virtually any problem. As an example, Kirst-Ashman and Hull (2001, p. 4) say that a generalist approach "means that virtually any problem may be analyzed and addressed from a number of perspectives that could potentially involve any size system."

Advocacy can be thought of as a specialized case of the generalist approach to solving problems. It is not the only method social workers use, but it is one of the techniques that makes social work unique among professions. Thus, all social workers should understand the principles and processes of advocacy.

The purpose of this book is to provide readers a concise but thorough understanding of advocacy: what it is, why to use it, and how to apply it in real life. I will present advocacy in the context of generalist social work practice. The main purpose of advocacy practice is the pursuit of social justice. This chapter introduces the stages of generalist social work practice and then describes advocacy practice as it relates to that approach to social work. It concludes with information about current trends in the field of social work.

A BRIEF REVIEW OF THE STAGES OF GENERALIST SOCIAL WORK PRACTICE

Various textbooks define generalist social work slightly differently. Common to all definitions, however, is that generalist social work practice consists of a series of stages that the social worker must work through. (If you are not familiar with the generalist approach to social work practice, a more thorough review can be found in several of the books listed in the reference section at the end of this book.)

Table 1.1 shows three conceptualizations of the generalist model as well as the corresponding steps of advocacy practice as presented in this book. Although the models of generalist practice are shown as linear processes, experience teaches that life does not always move smoothly or easily from one stage to another. Thus a social worker must remain flexible enough to recognize the process, step in at whichever stage is occurring, and approach the situation at the correct

TABLE 1.1 Phases of Generalist Social Work and Advocacy Practice

Generalist Social Work Practice			
Kirst-Ashman & Hull (1999)	*McMahon (1996)*	*Locke, Garrison, & Winship (1998)*	*Advocacy Practice*
Engagement	Engagement		Getting Involved
Assessment	Data Collection	Telling and Exploring the Story	Understanding the Issue
	Assessment		
Planning		Describing a Preferred Reality/Making Plans	Planning
Implementation	Intervention	Making Dreams Real	Advocating
Evaluation	Evaluation	Evaluating Outcomes	Evaluating
Termination	Termination	Making Transitions	
Follow-up			Ongoing Monitoring

Note: Because authors conceptualize the steps of generalist practice somewhat differently, this chart contains some empty cells.

3

level of intervention. Nevertheless, I present the stages as if they occur in a logical, straightforward way in order to simplify the learning process. In addition, I combine the authors' stages of generalist social work shown in table 1.1 to highlight their commonalities. In the following discussion, it is important to remember that the term *client* can refer to an individual, a group, an organization, or a community.

Stage 1: Engagement

Engagement is the first step of the generalist social work approach. It consists of getting to know the client and deciding to work with him or her. The relationship built at this time is the foundation for the rest of the social work intervention. The client must also choose to work with the social worker or else the process becomes something that is done to, rather than with, the client.

In the case of Ms. Jones, you already know the client but you may need to engage on the issue of her air conditioning being broken if it is new. She may not really want to work with you on this issue, looking instead for sympathy or a chance to vent. If you, as her social worker, are not careful, you may take her at face value when she says there is nothing that can be done. You may focus so much on your job duties that you neglect to listen and approach Ms. Jones and her family's plight with an eye toward advocacy.

Stage 2: Data Collection/Assessment

Once a joint decision to work together has been made, the next stage is to collect information about the client and assess the actual problem(s) to be worked on. Clients may have a presenting problem (what first got the client into contact with the social worker) that on further assessment is not the most important issue or the issue first addressed. Locke, Garrison, and Winship describe this stage as telling and exploring the story. This particular phrasing paints an amiable picture of active listening on the social worker's part, leading to understanding the client's perspective based on his or her narrative. The phrasing is meant to denote a strengths perspective, which leads social workers away from focusing only on clients' problems and helps them to see the client as a whole person. Perhaps the terms *data collection* and *assessment* do not sound as friendly. Nonetheless, this stage of the process is when client and social worker agree about which issues will be worked on. Proper data collection and assessment are vital to lay the groundwork for future steps in the helping process.

During this stage, the social worker needs knowledge of appropriate data collection and assessment instruments and techniques, a strong appreciation of social work values, and adeptness in listening to and questioning the client and others involved in the helping process. The social worker must be able to understand the client's views while also seeing matters from one or more other viewpoints.

An example of this technique in practice is the case of Ms. Jones, cited at the beginning of this chapter. In her frustration and anger at the air conditioning being broken, Ms. Jones blames her landlord for being "no good" and claims that nobody can help her. Although understanding her situation is important for the social worker, it would be of little help to Ms. Jones if the social worker agreed that nothing could be done to assist in making the living conditions better for her family. In fact, after appropriate listening and questioning to assess the situation accurately, the social worker may be able to come up with several ideas that could improve this client's future, both in the short-term and the long-term. This list could include emergency shelter assistance, electric fans or a "loaner" window air conditioning unit from a local charity, free passes to a city swimming pool, information on housing alternatives, legal help to force the landlord to provide air conditioning, information on tenants' rights and how to have a legal rent strike, and so on. These potential interventions do not adopt the client's perspective that the landlord is no good or that the situation cannot be improved, but rather bring up other perspectives to be considered.

Stage 3: Planning

Once data collection and assessment have been completed, the next stage is planning. Priorities and goals are set, and means to achieve goals are jointly discussed and decided upon. This stage is sometimes the most difficult to conduct because there is a desire by both the social worker and the client to "make things happen, now!" But without careful planning that relates client and social worker actions to goals and objectives, the end result too often is minimal accomplishment and maximal disillusionment. Goals and objectives can be created at all levels of social work intervention, depending on which level(s) seem most appropriate for the issue(s) being tackled.

In the case of Ms. Jones, planning could encompass several issues. One is the lack of air conditioning; another is her son's health; and a third is the overall condition of the apartment complex. Although the most obvious plan is to focus on the high temperatures in the apartment, planning and prioritizing among the possible goals for this client will help focus action now and in the future.

Stage 4: Implementation

After an advocate completes plans, implementation is the next stage. The most wonderful plans are worthless if they are not put into effect. Because even the best-laid plans often do not work out exactly as designed, core skills at this stage are the ability to be flexible, to roll with the punches, and to quickly develop alternate plans to achieve desired outcomes.

Continued measurement and assessment during the implementation stage allows everyone involved to see where progress is occurring and where it is not. Just as a United Way organization might use a "donations thermometer" to show how close the annual campaign is to meeting its fund-raising goal, social workers and clients should devise methods for keeping an eye on how close they are to achieving their goals and objectives.

You may plan with Ms. Jones to call the landlord of the apartment complex to advocate on her behalf. If the landlord is not available, or does not return your call, you must think of another option. Perhaps the city would see this as a violation of residential housing codes. Still, it will take time for the city inspectors to act. Keeping in mind your goals, which you decided with Ms. Jones, you may need to come up with other actions that help you to assist your client.

Stage 5: Evaluation

Evaluation means to determine the worth or effectiveness of an intervention. Without understanding what worked and what did not work, whether the intervention was counseling one client or implementing a policy affecting millions, learning cannot take place. Although many approaches to evaluation exist, it is vital to take steps to determine what happened during the implementation phase and what the results of the intervention were.

When you complete your intervention, take stock of your actions. In the Ms. Jones example, think of answers to these questions: Which actions worked? Which did not? What would you do differently if another client in a similar situation came to see you?

Stage 6: Termination

According to the generalist literature, social work interventions are finite and time-limited in nature. Social work values stress client self-determination and empowerment. Thus, social workers hope to work themselves out of a job. When clients are able to assess, plan, implement, and evaluate for themselves, the social worker can and should step out of the picture.

You may need to help Ms. Jones understand rental housing codes, what obligations landlords have to their tenants, and how she and her neighbors can work to prevent the need for your assistance in this type of situation.

Stage 7: Follow-up

Although not every text on generalist social work practice includes a follow-up stage, I include it here because it is important to know whether interventions are having a long-term effect. If clients cannot continue functioning well when social work support is withdrawn, something is amiss. Without follow-up, the true effectiveness of social work services cannot be determined, and we may then become guilty of continuing to use ineffective approaches to solve problems.

You might want to periodically check with Ms. Jones or others living in that apartment complex to determine if the air conditioning is still in working order. If the tenants have organized a council to represent them, you can ask if the air conditioning is functioning or inquire what the council is working on currently. Although this is not a formal follow-up, you will learn if your actions have had a lasting impact by asking a few simple questions.

AN INTRODUCTION TO ADVOCACY PRACTICE

Just as the generalist model of social work consists of various stages designed to solve client problems, advocacy practice is a problem-solving approach. This section first defines advocacy practice and then looks at the stages involved, noting how they are similar to the generalist practice approach described earlier.

Defining Advocacy Practice

Advocacy is a term with many definitions. Barker (1995, p. 11), in *The Social Work Dictionary*, defines *advocacy* as "the act of directly representing or defending others." The *Encyclopedia of Social Work* states that advocacy is "the act of directly representing, defending, intervening, supporting or recommending a course of action on behalf of one or more individuals, groups, or communities, with the goal of securing or retaining social justice (Mickelson, 1995, p. 95). Richan (1996) equates advocacy with lobbying. Jansson (2003) links the term *advocacy* to efforts to change policies in order to help relatively powerless groups. According to Gibelman and Kraft (1996, p. 46), "The many definitions of advocacy share in common an action orientation that is systematic and purposeful and which is undertaken to change some condition."

Advocacy practice is, then, that part of social work practice where the social worker takes action in a systematic and purposeful way to defend, represent, or otherwise advance the cause of one or more clients at the individual, group, organizational, or community level, in order to promote social justice. The usual targets of advocacy practice are decision makers in elected or appointed positions who create and legitimize laws, regulations, rules, and other types of policies, or decision makers who apply the policies others have created. These targets can be in government or in other organizations, such as nonprofits or businesses that make decisions that affect people's lives.

Advocacy practice is thus somewhat larger in scope than is the concept of "policy practice" used by Jansson (2003), because unlike policy practice, advocacy practice includes actions of social workers who do not necessarily try to change policy, but who insist on even-handed and just application of existing policy. This is similar to a lawyer arguing that the application of the law is invalid if used selectively against or in favor of one group or another. This type of advocacy against unfair decisions—for example, those made by street-level bureaucrats (Lipsky, 1980)—is an important element of advocacy prac-

8

tice. The great community organizer Saul Alinsky made a point of using an organization's rules against it by demanding that rules guaranteeing fair treatment were adhered to. He said, "Make the enemy live up to their own set of rules" (Alinsky, 1972, p. 10).

We turn now to the stages of advocacy practice, relating them to the analogous stages of generalist social work practice. Each of the stages is introduced here but has a separate chapter later in the book that explains it in greater detail.

Stage 1: Getting Involved

Such a large number of opportunities exist for people interested in advocacy, both in and out of their job settings, that the task of promoting social justice can sometimes seem so daunting as to make any effort merely a token one. As Margaret Mead once said, however, "Never doubt that a small group of committed individuals can change the world. It is the only thing that ever has."

The "getting involved" stage is analogous to the engagement stage of the generalist model of social work. The notion of getting involved implies a psychological readiness to expend energy, time, and possibly other resources in the pursuit of social justice, if only in the sense of helping one person be treated more fairly. Getting involved often stems from a sense of outrage about how someone or some group is being treated. Parents might become outraged at seeing their child unfairly affected by school policy, as when a head cheerleader was kept from participating in her extracurricular activity all semester for drinking off-campus, but a football player was removed from only one game for the same offense. A social worker might become outraged that gays and lesbians are declared ineligible for providing foster care or adopting because of their sexual orientation.

Other motivations are possible, too. Just as one of the most powerful predictors of volunteering is previous volunteer experience, present or future advocacy is often related to prior advocacy. Thus, even if the motivation for a person's first efforts at advocacy is to make a good grade in a class, to impress a potential partner, or to "feel a part of the action," there is likely no wrong motivation for advocacy in the name of social justice. In the end, continued advocacy is most likely linked to a person's ethical standards and sense of efficacy when employing advocacy practice skills. Therefore, it is important to understand the ethics of social justice (which will be covered in chap. 2) as well as to learn the most effective ways of acting as an advocate (which is examined in chaps. 3-9).

Stage 2: Understanding the Issues

Issues are situations and conditions that affect people. Some issues affect people positively, and some affect people negatively. Usually, though, situations and conditions affect some people positively and other people negatively. Although there are several steps to understanding an issue, the first is to figure out what the issue is. This task is both often overlooked and harder to do than expected. It is an overlooked step because the answer seems obvious—everybody knows that poverty, domestic violence, unemployment, and so on are issues with societal causes, except, of course, that some people believe these same problems are, at least in part, caused by individuals. Thus, particularly when people come at social justice issues from different value positions, the first step to understanding is to agree on a mutually acceptable definition of the problem to be addressed.

This step is harder to do than expected because of the difficulty in overcoming other people's, and our own, belief systems. Again, we may believe that the answer is obvious and be very surprised that another stance exists. Bridging the various viewpoints can be a challenge for advocates, but one that is necessary before moving to the next step in understanding the issue.

The second step is to determine who is being positively affected and who is being negatively affected by the identified issue. Poverty, for example, is an issue that has both positive and negative effects. It is, of course, a negative condition if you are a member of a family of four for which the income is below $16,000 per year. You are probably not eating nutritiously; your home, if you have one, is probably not well-made, and it probably needs repairs. You may live in a part of town that has inferior schools, poor access to public transit, and few job opportunities.

For those of us who are not poor, however, the condition has some positive elements. The existence of poverty means that wages in the United States can be held down to the minimum wage, or lower. This helps us to stretch our earnings further by making everyday items and the cost of eating out lower. Worldwide disparity in income is particularly helpful to us because so many things we like to own are made outside of our borders, where wages and working conditions are much worse than they are in the United States. Poverty, it may be argued, continues to exist in our country and around the world largely because it is such a positive condition for so many people.

Once it is clear who benefits and who loses from a particular condition or situation, the third step is to understand the causes of the issue. The issue of poverty, for example, has had many explanations for its existence. Some of the explanations have more evidence to support them than others.

Schiller (2004) describes three basic approaches for explaining poverty: flawed characters, restricted opportunities, and "big brother" government programs. Schiller decides, on the weight of the evidence, that the poor do not have flawed characters that inevitably lead them to lives of poverty. Government programs do perpetuate poverty for some people because of the way benefits are structured. Nonetheless, restricted opportunities in the workplace and in education, due to discrimination and macroeconomic policies created by government decisions, are the primary reasons poverty exists in the United States.

Other social issues often are explained in analogous ways. One faction believes the problem is caused by the individuals with the problem. Another faction believes external causes are primary. A third faction, which proposes that government programs are an important cause of the social problem, also may exist. Factions holding these views can often be labeled conservatives, liberals, and libertarians, respectively. Ideology is a filter through which information passes, and at times, advocates are so sure of the cause of an issue that they ignore information that contradicts their viewpoint. Although this certainly leads to consistent responses, it may also lead to incorrect understanding of an issue, which makes it important for social workers to understand and be aware of their own ideological tendencies.

The fourth step is to generate possible solutions to the issue. Trying to develop solutions truly helps us to understand the problem, because it forces us to show precisely how the actions that we may be able to take link to our perception of the issue. If we cannot explain how our plan can lead to the elimination of the problem, then we may not understand the problem well enough yet. It is a good idea to develop several possible solutions in this step so that you can choose the best solution for implementation.

The fifth step is to view the various proposed solutions and to determine how likely they are to lead to social justice. The basic approach to creating and looking at possible solutions is to ask the following questions repeatedly: What would be the results of adopting this solution? Who would be assisted? Who would be harmed? How would this solution act upon people currently affected negatively by this issue? How would this solution act upon people currently affected positively by this issue?

You should rank proposed solutions that lead to greater social justice higher in preference than ones that do not improve social justice as much. (Chap. 2 addresses what social justice is in greater detail.)

This stage, understanding the issues, in advocacy practice parallels the generalist model's data collection/assessment stage. In both cases, it is the prerequisite for the planning stage.

Stage 3: Planning

Planning is vital for effective advocacy practice. Based on their understanding of the issue, social workers and clients have developed possible solutions and chosen one to be the primary approach. This solution, if successfully adopted and implemented, will lead to greater social justice. Planning, then, is detailing the actions needed to make the preferred solution the one that is eventually chosen by decision makers, the targets of advocacy.

Step 1 of the planning stage is to identify what is wanted. This may seem easy, as the primary solution has been determined in stage 2, understanding the issues, but that is only the first part of the planning process. The overall solution, which might also be known as the advocacy goal or outcome, needs to be broken into smaller and more manageable outcomes, which in turn are connected to advocacy activities and participants. A tool called an advocacy map (see chap. 5) can be used to assist with moving from the "here" of a problematic situation to the "there" of a better future.

Step 2 in the planning process is to determine who the targets of advocacy are. Trying to influence people who have little or no say on the issue you wish to affect is a waste of time for everyone concerned. A state senator, for example, is not likely to assist in an effort to reallocate Community Development Block Grant funds. City council members in most cities, however, will be very active in making these decisions. Thus, it is vital to identify the decision maker(s) who can help you reach your goal.

Once you identify the targets, step 3 is to assess when you can or should act. Immediate action is not always possible, so it is important to lay the groundwork for later success, including finishing planning, making contacts, and gathering information.

Step 4 is to understand the way(s) that you can act so that you get what you want. This step requires an understanding of the principles of negotiation and persuasion. As decision makers tend to have strong individual preferences as to how they receive information, it may seem impossible to have general rules of how to negotiate and be convincing, but practice wisdom and research have made strides in both these areas.

Step 5 is to gather the appropriate information and incentives for bringing the target over to your side of the issue. The most important task of someone who wants to use advocacy to make a difference is to have information that is accurate and convincing. Most decision makers like to have not only tables of numbers and other facts but also case stories of how the issue is currently harming someone or examples of the kinds of people who would benefit from a change in policy. Proponents of abolishing the estate tax, for example, argued that heirs of family farmers and small business people were being harmed by selling their parents' farm or business in order to pay taxes on the inheritance. Opponents of removing the tax countered that people like Bill Gates (founder of Microsoft and world's wealthiest person) do not need to receive any tax relief. People on both sides of this argument had figures about the number of people affected by the decision and how their lives would be affected.

Once you know what you want, determine who the targets are, decide when to act, understand what the best ways to persuade are, and possess the information to be optimally convincing, the next stage is to put plans into action and actually advocate.

Stage 4: Advocating

This stage is where the planning pays off. Authors describing the generalist model have called this aspect of social work practice "implementation" (Kirst-Ashman & Hull, 1999), "intervention" (McMahon, 1996), and "making dreams real" (Locke, Garrison, & Winship, 1998). The common idea is that the social worker engages with the client in order to effect change.

The stage of advocating is when social workers may speak to a supervisor or board of directors, talk to legislators, call allies for action, write memos detailing grievances, or walk a picket line. You now put into effect the tactic(s) you chose during the planning stage. Change may occur quickly in some cases, although bigger changes and decisions often take years, if not decades, to make visible progress toward greater social justice.

Most social policy advocates understand the slow nature of true change. They keep one eye on the outcomes to be achieved and another eye on the present to ensure that plans are followed and conditions are assessed. Only by doing both can advocates truly make progress.

Stage 5: Evaluating

Advocacy practice performed without evaluation efforts is inadequate. People involved in change efforts must keep track of their level of success, whether the effort is aimed at changing the life of one person or one million people. Without the stimulus of an evaluation, even a fairly informal one, advocates will be less likely to examine why their efforts achieved what they did. Lessons for more skillful advocacy in the future can be derived from both success and failure. Learning, not assessing blame, is the goal of a healthy evaluation process. In general, evaluations use the planning documents created early in the advocacy effort to compare what was sought with what was achieved.

Stage 6: Ongoing Monitoring

Once evaluation determines that sufficient progress is being made, most social work texts indicate that termination of the helping relationship should occur. You should follow up at a later time to ensure that client progress is maintained. However, high caseloads do often prevent follow-up. In the advocacy practice model, termination rarely happens. In some ways, social workers who are advocates for social justice have taken on their issue(s) "until death do us part" because social justice is such a worthy, yet far-off, goal. Ongoing monitoring of specific conditions is required to provide information for new planning, new advocacy, and new evaluating.

Naturally, specific interventions with particular clients do terminate, even in advocacy practice. Advocates who do the job of training and empowering their clients can often step away, knowing that the former clients are now capable of advocating for themselves. Even so, social workers may wish to continue their quest for social justice in regard to one particular issue with other clients, in other communities, or at different levels of intervention. Ongoing monitoring is thus necessary to ensure effective advocacy.

The use of advocacy, whether conceived of as part of the generalist practice perspective or not, is also part of a larger context. The next section discusses four trends that affect the profession of social work and its use of advocacy.

THE BROADER CONTEXT FOR ADVOCACY PRACTICE

Four important trends affecting advocacy practice in the social work profession are explored in the next section. These trends are the rise in political behavior across the country, the requirements for evaluation of practice, the need for the measurement of practice outcomes, and the increasing need for maintaining and advancing basic elements of social justice.

The Rise in Political Behavior

Bucking a long downward spiral, Americans have recently become more interested in voting and other forms of political behavior. More than 122 million people voted in the 2004 presidential election, more than in any other campaign in American history and nearly 15 million more than just four years earlier. The percentage of eligible Americans voting in 2004 (nearly 61 percent) was the highest since 1968 when almost 68 percent voted. The increase in voter turnout between 2000 and 2004 (6.4 percent) was the highest increase between two presidential elections since 1952 (Faler, 2005).

15

The Internet is changing the way that people are learning about and following political behavior. "Fully 75 million Americans used the [I]nternet to get political news and information, discuss candidates and debate issues in emails, or participate directly in the political process by volunteering or giving contributions to candidates" (Rainie, Cornfield, & Horrigan, 2005, p. i). Nearly one-third of the general public and more than half of Internet users said they used the Internet to get news or information about the 2004 election, up from 18 percent and 33 percent, respectively, just four years earlier. People below the age of 50 were more likely to use the Internet (more than half), while those 50 years and older were less likely to use the Internet (Rainie et al.).

Advocacy practice does not always involve being active in campaigning or electoral politics. Still, once social workers see the need for advocacy at the case level, it is only a matter of time before the connections between what happens to individuals and the policies that create or shape the individual's problems becomes clear. At that point, the importance of politics and advocacy cannot be ignored.

The increased polarization of American politics is making for more extreme policy choices by legislators. In recent years, most policy changes have caused a decrease in government funding and support for social programs. These decisions quickly trickle down into the lives of clients, making programs less able to respond to client needs. With a sagging economy and struggling nonprofit sector, clients' lives are becoming harder. Social workers, whether initially interested in politics or not, rapidly see the effects of political wins and losses and so become more convinced to advocate for clients' needs at every level, including within the political system. The rise in political interest and behavior throughout the United States is surely affecting individual social workers and those who support social work values.

Still, we must remember that not all who have recently become active in politics share the ideals of the social work profession. It thus is important for social workers and their supporters to be aware of the best ways to conduct advocacy.

Requirements for the Evaluation of Practice

One of the key movements throughout the field of social work is the evaluation of practice, whether at the individual case level or at the program level. The term *evidence-based practice*, while still somewhat controversial, is increasingly used to describe social work practice that has been evaluated as being effective. The knowledge base being developed in order to show the efficacy of social work interventions is based on increasingly rigorous research (Briggs & Rzepnicki, 2004; Roberts & Yeager, 2004). Advocacy, however, is in a primitive place in terms of the development of an ethos of evidence-based practice— indeed, evaluation of advocacy efforts is a topic almost unmentioned in most social work practice texts, even those primarily directed at helping students and practitioners to improve their advocacy skills. This book provides research-based information whenever possible to guide the advocate in the promotion of social justice.

Need for Measurement of Practice Outcomes

The delineation and measurement of outcomes is related to the requirement to evaluate practice. Evaluation is often considered, at its core, an assessment of the degree to which an intervention achieved its desired outcomes. Without predetermined outcomes that can be measured, it is impossible to evaluate. Little has been done in the advocacy literature to bring a focus to measurable outcomes. Although it is common to note the importance of knowing what you want before entering into an advocacy situation, little attention has been paid to a systematic effort to measure, and thus be able to evaluate, the effects of the advocacy. (I cover this topic extensively in chap. 8.)

Increasing Need for Maintaining and Advancing Social Justice

Social justice is under attack. It is under attack in families, groups, organizations, cities, counties, states, the nation, and throughout the world. It is under attack every day. Although social workers do not have a monopoly on good ideas or the correct set of values, the profession of social work has firm ideas about the values that should dominate the decision-making process and the outcomes that should be achieved through individual and social action. Victories do occur and should be celebrated. Clients do receive more equal treatment, agency budget cuts are reduced or reversed, and social policy is made on the basis that people do matter, particularly those on the bottom of the economic and social ladder. Yet, too often, the advocates for increased concentration of power, wealth, and prestige win. One reason for this outcome is that social workers do not know how to advocate well for their clients and for themselves and their agencies. The core premise of this book is that *knowledge is power*—that knowledge of how to engage in a structured approach to advocacy will lead to more successful advocacy. This success, in turn, will lead to greater social justice across the country and perhaps even the world. We must all do our part, and the first step is to know what to do.

CONCLUSION

Social work practice of all types is frequently understood as a problem-solving process. Many authors have labeled the core components of social work practice as "generalist practice" because it can be used with clients of all types and at different levels of intervention, from the individual to the international.

This chapter has examined briefly several models of generalist social work practice. It introduces the idea of advocacy practice, which is conceptualized as a specialized form of social work practice with stages that parallel the generalist problem-solving approach. And it gives an overview of the six stages of advocacy practice—getting involved, understanding the issues, planning, advocating, evaluation, and monitoring.

I also describe four trends in order to provide a larger context for studying and applying advocacy practice. These trends—the rise in political behavior, the requirements for the evaluation of practice, the need to measure outcomes, and the increasing need for maintaining and advancing social justice—are connected to the formulation of advocacy practice. Laying the groundwork for the rest of the book, this overview allows readers to understand the place of advocacy practice in the big picture of generalist social work practice. In the next chapter, I examine social justice—the goal of advocacy practice—in detail.

Suggested Further Reading

Jansson, B. (2003). *Becoming an effective policy advocate: From policy practice to social justice* (4th ed.). Pacific Grove, CA: Brooks/Cole.

This textbook first identified advocacy and working within the policy-making arena as an area of social work practice equal with other types of social work practice. The text organizes a massive amount of information pertaining to politics, policy-making, and social work advocacy.

Perlman, H. (1957). *Casework: A problem solving process.* Chicago: University of Chicago Press.

This book, a true classic, has sold over 200,000 copies and has been translated into at least ten languages. Adhering to neither the Freudian nor the Rankian approach to clinical practice prevalent at the time, Perlman relied on her social work experience and keen mind to reject long-term psychotherapy as a model for social work practice. Instead, she developed social casework, a short-term approach based on the idea that a person comes to a place with a problem that often needs to be broken into solvable pieces. Solving one piece of the client's problems often led to gains in other areas as well. Perlman's approach is still the backbone of social work practice.

Chapter 2

SOCIAL JUSTICE AND
ADVOCACY PRACTICE

*"Social workers have a professional responsibility to make ... choices
and to participate in the broader societal debate to resolve issues of
social change."* (Iatridis, 1994, p. 203)

Mara Liasson, reporter for National Public Radio, started a presentation to a National Association of Social Workers Political Action Institute by defining her subject. The word *politics*, she said, "comes from *polis*, a Greek word meaning community, and *tics*, meaning small, bloodsucking insects. Politics is thus a domain of life controlled by a group of people leeching off the rest of us." Unfortunately for the field of social work and the United States at large, this facetious definition is widely accepted.

The belief that politics and thus advocacy is a dirty arena, populated by the worst kinds of people, and something that no decent person would want to be associated with, is all too common in social work. There is, however, another view of politics. A political scientist, Harold Lasswell, wrote that politics is the process by which it is decided "who gets what, when and how" (1936). This view of politics as process is echoed in a social work policy text that states, "Whether it is the product of governmental, voluntary, or corporate institutions, welfare policy is concerned with allocating goods, services, and opportunities in order to enhance social functioning" (Karger & Stoesz, 2005, p. 3). Politics, in this view, is simply a tool that can be used for good or bad purposes.

A similar, though simplified, version of this definition is politics (or policy making) is deciding how stuff gets spread around. The *only* question, then, is whether social workers (or any other group of individuals with common interests) want to help make these decisions or not. If you are not the decision maker yourself, then advocacy is the process by which you help make the decisions on these matters. Former Texas state senator and current mayor of Fort Worth, Texas, Mike Moncrief is fond of saying that social workers and politicians have a common goal: to help people. Barbara Mikulski, United States senator from Maryland, says, "Politics is simply social work with power" (Reisch, 1995, p. 1). If social workers want to assist clients, it is imperative that enough of them are active and capable advocates in the policy-making arena to ensure that things happen:

> We are now making fundamental political decisions about our society: choices which literally involve matters of life and death, health and illness, opportunity and oppression, hope and despair, for millions of people. These choices are integral to the core concerns of social work as a profession and to our integrity as caring human beings. They have a major impact on the lives of our clients and the day-to-day work we do in our agencies and communities. They require us to make political action a central, ongoing component of our work, to abandon the false image of professionalism which separates professional responsibilities from the harsh realities of poverty, power, and politics. (Reisch, 1995, p. 1)

Social workers must be involved in advocacy practice if clients' situations are to improve. If social workers do not act as advocates, their policy ideas and, even more importantly, their *values* will not be well represented in policy-making circles. When social workers engage in advocacy practice, they bring with them specialized knowledge about the human condition and a belief that service provision to clients must consider individuals within their environment. Social workers also want to focus on client strengths, rather than pathology. When social workers share their knowledge and beliefs, decision makers are exposed to a fresh point of view.

Decision makers are encountered in many different places—not just in the legislative branch of the government or in the top strata of other organizations. Decision makers can be found everywhere in organizations because even low-level workers have to interpret ambiguous regulations, rules, and customs in their place of employment. Organizational culture may make some choices the "obvious" one, even if it runs counter to client interests. These decisions are just as appropriate for advocacy practice as is passing a law.

Because values are such an important component of social workers' advocacy practice, it is important to identify the source of these values. The next section looks at the National Association of Social Workers' professional code of ethics to explore the connection between professional responsibility (as defined in the Code) and advocacy practice.

ADVOCACY IN THE NATIONAL ASSOCIATION OF SOCIAL WORKERS' CODE OF ETHICS

According to social worker and member of the Detroit city council, Maryanne Mahaffey, "What the social worker brings [to the advocacy process] is a value system that, if implemented, along with the [proper] skills, makes the difference" (Haynes & Mickelson, 2000, p. 40). One of the best places to look at the values used to justify advocacy practice is in the Code of Ethics of the primary professional organization of social workers in the United States, the National Association of Social Workers.

There are several parts of the Code of Ethics (last revised in 1999) which indicate that being involved in advocacy is one part of a professional social worker's job description. This idea is stated most clearly in Section 6.01:

> Social workers should promote the general welfare of society, from local to global levels, and the development of people, their communities, and their environment. Social workers should advocate for living conditions conducive to the fulfillment of basic human needs and should promote social, economic, political, and cultural values and institutions that are compatible with the realization of social justice. (National Association of Social Workers [NASW], 1999)

The Code further explains this responsibility in Section 6.04:

22

(a) Social workers should engage in social and political action that seeks to ensure that all people have equal access to the resources, employment, services, and opportunities they require to meet their basic human needs and to develop fully. Social workers should be aware of the impact of the political arena on practice and should advocate for changes in policy and legislation to improve social conditions in order to meet basic human needs and promote social justice.

(b) Social workers should act to expand choice and opportunity for all persons, with special regard for vulnerable, disadvantaged, oppressed, and exploited people and groups. (NASW, 1999)

The Code addresses involving the public in politics in Section 6.02: "Social workers should facilitate informed participation by the public in shaping social policies and institutions" (NASW, 1999). Thus, social workers not only have an obligation to participate actively in advocacy themselves, but also to empower others to do so as well. Social work administrators have a specific duty along these lines, too, according to the 1999 Code of Ethics; Section 3.07(a) declares, "Social work administrators should advocate within and outside their agencies for adequate resources to meet clients' needs."

Despite the specificity and clarity of the 1999 Code of Ethics, a frequent concern in the literature is that social workers do not have the skills necessary to be policy advocates and to encourage others to shape social policy (Wolk, 1981). Many blame this situation on social work education programs' lack of student training in these skills (Ezell, 1993; Haynes & Mickelson, 2000; Mary, Ellano, & Newell, 1993). Recent years have seen a small increase in the number of courses on political social work (Haynes & Mickelson, 2000), including a specialization in the topic at the University of Houston and a formal legislative internship program at the University of Texas at Arlington, which includes a course on politics and social work and an internship in a state legislator's district office. Still, few field placements are available in political settings (Wolk, Pray, Weismiller, & Dempsey, 1996).

Despite the lack of formal advocacy skills training for social work students, it is important for you to continue to seek knowledge about advocacy and learn its place in the profession. The next section examines what social workers are trying to accomplish with their efforts.

SOCIAL JUSTICE IN THE NASW CODE OF ETHICS

The 1999 NASW Code of Ethics sets forth six core values of the profession: service, social justice, dignity and worth of the person, importance of human relationships, integrity, and competence. A complete description of these values is beyond the scope of this book, but it is important to take a closer look at the value of social justice because it is the value that most encourages advocacy practice.

In the section titled Ethical Principles, the Code of Ethics states that "Social workers challenge social injustice" (NASW, 1999). The Code immediately elaborates on what this principle means by declaring:

> Social workers pursue social change, particularly with and on behalf of vulnerable and oppressed individuals and groups of people. Social workers' social change efforts are focused primarily on issues of poverty, unemployment, discrimination, and other forms of social injustice. These activities seek to promote sensitivity to and knowledge about oppression and cultural and ethnic diversity. Social workers strive to ensure access to needed information, services, and resources; equality of opportunity, and meaningful participation in decision making for all people. (NASW, Ethical Principles)

The NASW Code explicitly mentions some of the main, concrete issues for social workers wanting to work for greater social justice. The concept of social justice is difficult to define, however, as it means different things to different people. Making matters difficult for social workers who want to follow the Code of Ethics' call to work for social justice is that the Code does not define the term and there is no entry for it, or related terms, in *The Social Work Dictionary* (Barker, 1995). The *Encyclopedia of Social Work*'s entry for "Social Justice in Social Agencies" does not define the term *social justice* either (Flynn, 1995). Fortunately, Van Soest (1995) provides some help in her *Encyclopedia of Social Work* entry for "Peace and Social Justice." She indicates that three views of social justice exist. *Legal justice*, the first view, is concerned with what a person owes to society. *Commutative justice*, the second view, is concerned with what people owe each other. *Distributive justice*, the third view, is concerned with what society owes a person. Of these three views, the most applicable to a social work approach to social justice is distributive justice.

DISTRIBUTIVE JUSTICE

One of the most important elements of the struggle over social welfare policy is the difference in interpretation of the term *distributive justice*. Distributive justice "concerns the justified distribution of benefits and burdens in society....The distribution of benefits and burdens is a cooperative social process structured by various moral, legal, ideological, and cultural principles" (Iatridis, 1994, p. 62). Thus, politics, "the process of distributing stuff," is the way that distributive justice either is or is not made a reality; therefore, the debates of political philosophers deserve considerable attention from social workers (Reamer, 1993).

Although many variations of belief exist, there are two major contemporary viewpoints about distributive justice in the United States. On the one hand are people who believe that distributive justice means that resources should be spread relatively evenly across the entire citizenry as a matter of right. This view has been called the "egalitarian view" (Van Soest, 1995, p. 1811) and the "fairness model" (Iatridis, 1994, p. 67). On the other hand are those who believe that an unequal distribution of resources is better because it reflects differences in ability and effort. This belief has been called the "libertarian view" (Van Soest, p. 1811) and the "market model" (Iatridis, p. 64).

Although the literature on this topic is extensive, two modern philosophers' writings exemplify these different viewpoints. John Rawls and Robert Nozick each penned very influential works on the subject of distributive justice in the early 1970s. Their different interpretations of the concept have provided a great deal of material for debate since that time.

John Rawls's Views on Distributive Justice

Rawls (1971) asks his readers to imagine that they are going to develop the rules for a society knowing that people will be randomly "assigned" different places in society once the "game of life" begins. Participants in this thought experiment must agree ahead of time to live within the rules they develop, but they do not know what position in society they are going to be given, what Rawls calls "the veil of ignorance." A person may be assigned a position among the wealthy elite, with many resources and privileges, or the participant may be among those with very little material resources. However, for this type of inequality to exist, the rules agreed to have to allow for the inequality. Given this veil of ignorance about one's future assigned position in society, Rawls argues that people will want to create the fairest set of rules possible, if only to protect themselves from being placed into a very difficult situation. According to Rawls, this set of "the fairest possible rules" would be based on two main principles. The first principle is that "each person is to have an equal right to the most extensive total system of equal basic liberties compatible with a similar system of liberty for all" (Rawls, p. 302). This ensures that all are treated equally within the context of the rules, which are addressed in the second principle. This principle states that "social and economic inequalities are to be arranged so that they are both (a) to the greatest benefit of the least advantaged and (b) attached to offices and positions open to all under considerations of fair equality of opportunity" (Rawls, p. 302).

The second principle is an especially important point. Inequality is not seen as an evil in and of itself, but rather as a condition that can be harnessed for the good of all. An example may help illustrate the idea. The rules set forth under the veil of ignorance might allow some positions in society to be more appealing than others, such as those with higher pay, better working conditions, and so on. In the case of physicians, for example, we want very capable practitioners because they make life-and-death decisions that require considerable levels of skill and many years of difficult training. Because there are a limited number of people with the required aptitude and because the training process is arduous, members of society may encourage everyone with the requisite aptitude to fill those positions in society rather than taking them themselves. Furthermore, people who become physicians could earn more than others without breaking the second principle if they are required to use some of their time to assist the least advantaged in society. Point b, above, ensures, moreover, that the position of physician is open to everyone with the appropriate aptitude and is not limited by reasons of race, gender, social class, or other non-merit considerations.

Rawls's approach to distributive justice has considerable appeal to many social workers. Those who have tried to figure out how to apply his principles quickly run into practical difficulties, however. No matter which set of rules is agreed to under the veil of ignorance, even when using Rawls's two principles, it is difficult to determine whether that structure is "to the *greatest* benefit of the *least* advantaged" and, therefore, "just."

Robert Nozick's Views on Distributive Justice

A very different interpretation of distributive justice is set forth by Robert Nozick (1974) in *Anarchy, State and Utopia*. Nozick argues that Rawls, and others, who focus on "end-states" or "patterns" of a distributive process are wrong. In order to maintain a "fair" distribution of resources, a central distribution mechanism would have to exist, and it does not. In other words, the end-state, or the point at which people have been assigned their positions and given the rules, is theoretically a rather equal distribution of economic goods. However, the distribution is constantly made less equal because people put forth unequal effort and have unequal skills and under Rawls's system are paid according to effort and skill. The only way to prevent inequality is to have government redistribute wealth constantly.

> In a free society, diverse persons control different resources, and new holdings arise out of the voluntary exchanges and actions of persons. There is no more a distributing or distribution of shares than there is a distributing of mates in a society in which persons choose whom they shall marry. The total result is the product of many individual decisions which the different individuals involved are entitled to make (Nozick, pp. 149-150).

The proposed solution is a procedural approach to distributive justice in which "a distribution is just if everyone is entitled to the holdings he possesses under the distribution" (Nozick, 1974, p. 151). To simplify this theory, "From each as they choose, to each as they are chosen" (Nozick, p. 160).

An example illustrates his approach clearly. An "end-state" theorist might object to a distribution of income that left many people with little and a few (including sports stars) with much. But suppose that "the many" choose to buy tickets to football games where the stars play. The football team makes a large profit and pays the players quite well. Nozick argues that this voluntary transfer of holdings (income) from the many to the few is completely just and that any move to redistribute it through governmental action (coercion) is unjust. He makes this last point very strongly when he states, "Taxation of earnings from labor is on a par with forced labor" (p. 169).

Under Nozick's approach, the main principle to ensure social justice, then, is to set up a way for fair, voluntary exchanges to take place. This market should be as unfettered as possible. Once the rules are set and followed, any end result, no matter how unequal, is socially just. Government's major duty is to ensure that fair rules are followed, because that enforcement leads to a just outcome. The idea is similar to political freedom. As long as the rules of one-person, one-vote are followed in an election and everyone has a chance to vote, the result of such a free election is just and fair. It is not just, however, to determine who should win an election ahead of time in order to have a "fair" distribution of elected positions, meaning that they are given to different types of people. Similarly, it is not just to determine if the outcome of an economic distribution is fair by looking at the amount of inequality that ensues. As long as fair rules are followed in the marketplace, the distribution of money that results is just.

Comparing Rawls's and Nozick's Views

The practical implications of these two interpretations of the term *distributive justice* vary greatly. Nozick's formulation would eliminate many, if not all, government efforts at redistribution and would return the country to a system where charity giving was the only support for people who could not earn their own living. This harsh state of affairs would mean that social work values would be under great duress. Inequality would certainly be increased. It is a very individualistic approach to how society should operate, although it is consistent with many of the basic tenets of American values.

Rawls's viewpoint requires many calculations to be made that may be beyond most persons' abilities, but the general thrust of his approach is congruent with social work values. The approach focuses on the least advantaged members of society and seeks to improve their condition. Despite the practical difficulties of determining the exact level of "justness" that is involved in any one situation, it is clear that the NASW Code of Ethics is also written with an eye on the needs of the least advantaged members of society. This viewpoint, too, has a place among American values but is clearly not the dominant value. Nonetheless, the Rawlsian view is the dominant value amongst social workers:

> [the view] supports the normative aspects of social policy practice and the ethical commitments of social work. It emphasizes humanness and the enhancement of being human. It also promotes welfare-state programs that redistribute goods and services in favor of the poor, the disadvantaged, and populations at risk (Iatridis, 1994, p. 69).

WHAT ARE SOCIAL WORKERS TRYING TO ACCOMPLISH WITH ADVOCACY?

It is all well and good to be an advocate: indeed, some might argue that a democratic society needs people to be active simply because engagement in the process is good. Social work, however, takes a normative view of what the desired outcomes of the advocacy process should be. Many purposes for social work advocacy are listed in the NASW Code of Ethics. Meeting client needs, both material and emotional, should be uppermost in the minds of social worker advocates. And their goal should be to end exploitation, oppression, and discrimination. These are lofty goals, and one may wonder if social workers actually believe in these values.

Research by Abbott (1988) indicates that social workers consistently rank higher than other professional groups in their belief in four important social work values: respect for basic rights, sense of social responsibility, commitment to individual freedom, and support for self-determination. This is true even for beginning graduate students, as compared to students in other professional programs (Abbott, p. 44). Social work students, at both the BSW and MSW levels, "report high levels of social work idealism" in response to the following statements: (1) "Access to opportunities and resources should be open to all" and (2) "Social workers have an obligation to advocate for change in their communities" (Csikai & Rozensky, 1997, p. 537). The mean scores on these statements indicate that social work students "agree" to "strongly agree" with these ideas.

There was a shift in social workers' attitudes toward poverty and social action between 1968 and 1984 (Reeser & Epstein, 1987). Surprisingly, respondents in 1984 were more likely both to believe that poverty was due to structural factors and to be less committed to activist goals than were social workers in 1968. This shift in attitude may have two causes: (1) casework and psychotherapy becoming the primary social work methods and (2) a sense of futility about social change due to the insensitivity of the Reagan administration toward social work concerns.

In summary, it appears that social workers may, in fact, believe in social work values, at least more so than people in other professional groups. This finding underscores the importance of social workers engaging in advocacy practice because their beliefs and values are unique. Interestingly, however, Csikai and Rozensky (1997) also found that the social work students surveyed had comparatively little agreement with statements such as "Advocacy is the main thrust of social work" and "Social workers' responsibilities should include active involvement in lobbying for political change." Both of these statements had a mean score placing them between "uncertain" and "agree" on the scale used. Perhaps most disturbing for those who see a strong need for advocacy practice because of the impact of policy decisions on social work practice, students in this study indicate considerable agreement with the statement "Political issues have no bearing on direct social work practice with individuals" (Csikai & Rozensky, p. 533). Thus, although social workers and social work students agree with the values of social work, members of these groups may be unwilling or unable to use advocacy practice in making social work values become part of social policy in their nation, state, county, city, or agency.

EXAMPLES OF ETHICAL ISSUES IN ADVOCACY PRACTICE

Up to now, this chapter has focused on the ethical responsibility social workers have to address societal and client problems through advocacy and the need to focus on social justice in their practice. Still, the question remains, *How do these principles operate in the "real world"?* Is everything fair in love, war, and advocacy practice, or should social workers be held to some other standard of behavior?

Saul Alinsky (1971, p. 25), in his classic essay "Of Means and Ends," argues forcefully that people who extensively debate the morality of means and ends "wind up on their ends without any means." Organizers must use what is available to enable them to accomplish their goals: "He who sacrifices the mass good for personal salvation has a peculiar conception of 'personal salvation'; he doesn't care enough for people to be 'corrupted' for them" (Alinsky, p. 25). It is appropriate to be concerned with ethics only when there is a choice of means. Thus, if the ends are just and the means are limited to one tactic, that tactic, no matter what it is, is fair. It is only the powerful who call the effective tactics of the dispossessed "unfair" (Alinsky).

The NASW Code of Ethics may be used to support Alinsky's view in part, but the overall message is clear that social workers should be held accountable to a higher standard. Maryanne Mahaffey maintains this point vigorously:

> There are people who tell me that the ends justify the means. This is antithetical to social work values. . . . For social workers the ends and the means must be consistent. Another way to put it: If the method you use to arrive at your ends are [sic] dirty, then the end result will be dirty. (Haynes and Mickelson, 2000, p. 52)

Although social workers are called upon to engage in advocacy practice, the Code is often silent on the subject of how to do so ethically. In addition, there appear to be some contradictions inherent in

31

the Code. The very first sentence of the detailed ethical standards states plainly, "Social workers' primary responsibility is to promote the welfare of clients. In general, clients' interests are primary" (NASW, 1999, Sec. 1.01). This is immediately followed, however, by the statement, "However, social workers' responsibility to the larger society or specific legal obligations may on limited occasions supersede the loyalty owed clients . . . " (NASW, Sec. 1.01). Reporting child abuse is given as a specific example of when loyalty to the client is overcome by legal obligations.

The fifth ethical principle described in the Code is *Integrity*. Social workers must be "continually aware of the profession's mission, values, ethical principles, and ethical standards" and to "practice in a manner consistent with them." More specifically, "Social workers act honestly and responsibly and promote ethical practices on the part of the organizations with which they are affiliated." Honesty is certainly an important element in being effective in advocacy efforts, but is honesty always the best policy? Is it permissible to lie if it better accomplishes social work's primary mission to "enhance human well-being and help meet basic human needs, with particular attention to the needs of vulnerable, oppressed and poor people" (NASW 1999, Preamble)?

There are no firm answers to these questions. At best we can do what Jansson (1994, p. 59) suggests to do when ethical principles conflict:

> When issues reflect important values and consequences, they should not be resolved impulsively. We should feel tugged in different directions, as if each alternative is serious and cannot be lightly dismissed. Were we to hurriedly resolve such issues, we might later decide that we had compromised important values and overlooked important consequences.

In the end, "reasonable differences of opinion exist among social workers" (NASW, 1999, Sec. 3.10[b]). Not every social worker will come up with the same solution to a problem. Still, "Social workers should carefully examine relevant issues and their possible impact on clients before deciding on a course of action" (NASW, Sec. 3.10[b]).

The following are some examples of situations for which there are no clear answers, and reasonable social workers may indeed disagree on how to proceed.

You are chair of a statewide social work political action committee. A major newspaper writes a disturbing story on Maria Rodriguez, a candidate your committee has already endorsed for state senator in the primary race, which she won. The report says that she has falsified her academic credentials. Ms. Rodriguez first denies, then admits, the deception. The committee did not endorse this candidate based on her academic record, but rather for the twenty years of good work she has completed on behalf of low-income Mexican Americans in south Texas. Some of the members of your political action committee want to continue as if nothing has happened—"Her strong voice is needed in the state senate to protect against conservatives of both parties!" Others want to renounce the earlier endorsement and ask her to remove herself from the race altogether—"She lied to us!" A third group thinks it best to express disappointment in her, but support her privately—"She let us down, but she is still the better of the two available candidates."

You are asked by your state NASW chapter to help organize a "get out the vote" drive in your city because you have done similar work with the League of Women Voters, a nonpartisan group. You are willing to do this, as you believe that "social workers should facilitate informed participation by the public" (NASW, 1999, Section 6.02). The main organizers are clear, however, that the vote they want to get out consists of only registered Democrats, as Democratic voters are much more likely to vote for Democratic candidates than are members of other parties or nonaffiliated voters. When you object, the organizer explains that Laura Smith, the Democratic candidate, is pro-choice while the Republican candidate in the race is antiabortion. Ms. Smith has also been endorsed by the NASW. "The Christian Coalition and Moral Majority are mobilizing their forces to get out only Republican voters," says the organizer. "Why shouldn't we do the same for our side?" Although you understand this logic, you are still not convinced that this is entirely ethical for NASW, which is officially a nonpartisan group.

You are a longtime member of NASW and consider yourself a political conservative. You believe that NASW is too liberal and especially disagree with its pro-welfare position. You are convinced that, despite changes to end "old-style" welfare, the welfare system created a generation of people who believe that they are entitled to public support. Even with the threat of being cut off from government assistance, some able-bodied recipients and their children have little hope of becoming self-sufficient because the aid they receive from charities and government eliminates incentives for gainful employment. Although you don't mind having a different opinion about policy compared to most social workers, you have noticed (starting in graduate school) a tendency for conservative social workers to be frozen out of social circles. This is a problem for you because you want to keep on other social workers' good side because your practice relies on their referrals. Should you remain in the organization and try to change its policies to be more in line with your values, should you remain a member of NASW to keep the good insurance benefits available to members but otherwise quietly work against its proposals, or should you give up your membership because of your philosophical differences with the organization?

A client of yours in a nonprofit agency could make good use of a special fund set aside for buying back-to-school clothes. When you mention this to your supervisor, she agrees but cautions you to provide only half the allowed amount of funds in order to keep money available for other clients. You believe that special circumstances make it vital to assist your client with more than half the amount possible. Yet you know that there are limited funds for this purpose. You are also aware that your six-month probationary period still has two months to go. Social work jobs as good as this one are hard to come by in your small community. What should you do?

In order to address situations such as the one above in a systematic way, first choose which ethical principles are in conflict. Refer specifically to the NASW Code of Ethics and other ethical codes that may apply, such as those that cover licensed social workers in your state. Ask which principle, in this situation, is more important. Gather opinions from other social workers you trust. In the end, you may need to prioritize one principle over another in order to resolve the conflict.

CONCLUSION

Using advocacy to promote social justice is every social worker's responsibility. The NASW Code of Ethics makes this responsibility clear. Every social worker must then understand what is meant by the different views of social justice and be able and willing to support the definition most in line with social work values.

Social workers have important information about client needs and a distinctive view of social justice. Social workers tend to believe that people at the bottom of economic and social ladders should be helped to climb more quickly than people who are already higher on the ladder.

The rest of this book covers the most effective ways to advocate for these values to be adopted by decision makers and thus translated into laws and regulations. Each chapter covers one of the steps in advocacy practice. The final chapter summarizes and brings together the lessons from the book.

Suggested Further Reading

Iatridis, D. (1994). *Social policy: Institutional context of social development and human services.* Pacific Grove, CA: Brooks/Cole.

This fairly small and pithy book has an excellent discussion of the role of national value systems and how they affect social policy. Advocates working within an understanding of the values of their institutional context will be more effective than those without such an understanding.

Lasswell, H. (1936). *Politics: Who get what, when, and how.* New York: Free Press.

Although this is an older book, it still enlightens any discussion of politics. Lasswell, a psychologist who studied political communication and propaganda techniques, begins the book stating that, "The study of politics is the study of influence and the influential" (p. 3). The remainder of the book justifies this position. The second chapter, about the use of political symbols, is still astonishingly illuminating and easy to apply to current political concerns.

Chapter 3

GETTING INVOLVED

"Politics ought to be the part-time profession of every citizen who would protect the rights and privileges of free people and who would preserve what is good and fruitful in our national heritage."(Eisenhower, 1954)

According to the generalist social work practice model described in chapter 1, the first step of the helping process is "engagement." In advocacy practice, the first step is labeled "getting involved." This chapter examines the research on why people get involved in political action and then extends the conclusions to why people become involved in advocacy, whether they are advocating for one individual or thousands.

Getting involved requires a decision to be made, a choice between doing nothing and doing something. Although motivation varies from one person to the next, research indicates that several prerequisites are usually in place before the choice is made to do something. Although the research cited here refers mainly to being active in politics on a macroscale, the same thinking process and prerequisites need to occur no matter what level of advocacy is being undertaken. The next section looks explicitly at political activism, but later in the chapter I extend the discussion to advocacy in general.

WHY ARE SOME PEOPLE ACTIVE IN POLITICS?

All is not well in the American political system. Political cynicism is rampant, and trust in government may be at an all-time low. One of the more popular beliefs about politics is that people in other industrialized democratic countries are more active than those in the United States. This belief is not entirely true historically or currently. There is considerable political activity in the United States, especially in an international context. Voter turnout, as a percentage of the eligible population, *is* relatively low in the United States, but Americans are more active in other ways: they are active members of local groups that are working on community problems, working for a political party, or contacting officials about problems. Still, people often ask why Americans are not more active in politics. This section addresses a different question: why *is* anybody active in politics?

In his classic study *Who Governs?*, Robert Dahl (1961) wrote about two types of people: *homo civicus* and *homo politicus. Homo civicus* is "civic man," who is not, by nature, a political animal. This type of person may become active in politics when danger is perceived, "but when the danger passes, homo civicus may usually be counted on to revert to his normal preoccupation with nonpolitical strategies for attaining his primary goals" (Dahl, p. 225). *Homo politicus,* or "political man," on the other hand, "deliberately allocates a very sizable share of his resources to the process of gaining and maintaining control over the policies of government" (Dahl, p. 225). Why do most people turn into *homo civicus* and only a few into *homo politicus?* The best explanation Dahl provides is that "some individuals find that political action is a powerful source of gratification" (Dahl, p. 225). More recent research, while not disputing this psychological approach, provides additional theories about why people do or do not get involved in politics.

Milbrath (1965) also classifies the American public according to three levels of participation: the apathetic, spectators, and gladiators. A large number (about 33 percent) of Americans are apathetic, but even this is a type of political activity. These people generally obey laws but otherwise do not expose themselves to political stimuli and are generally unaware of the political world.

The largest group (nearly 60 percent) is made up of spectators. These people do participate in basic civic activities but do little else. They vote, they may initiate political discussions, and they sometimes try to sway the votes of family and friends. Spectators might also wear a political button or display a bumper sticker on their car.

A very small number (no more than 7 percent) of the American public are gladiators who live and breathe politics (Milbrath, 1965). Activities in which they participate include contributing time to a political campaign, becoming an active party member, attending a caucus, soliciting political funds, and running for or holding public office, in addition to spectator activities. "A very small band of gladiators battle fiercely to please the spectators, who have the power to decide their fate" (Milbrath, p. 20).

Other political activities, such as contacting a public official, contributing money to a party or candidate, and attending a political meeting or rally, are "transitional activities" that spectators begin to engage in when their level of interest carries them toward becoming gladiators (Milbrath, 1965).

Four different factors lead to different levels of political behavior (Milbrath, 1965, p. 38). The first is the nature and level of the stimuli reaching the potential political actor. These stimuli can be thought of first as what is present in the environment and second as what stimuli actually reach the consciousness of the individual after passing through whatever perceptual screens are in place. A person's values are what allow stimuli to reach his or her consciousness. The second factor is the personal attributes of the individual, including attitudes, beliefs, knowledge, and personality traits. The third factor is the nature of the political system, which by its rules includes some and excludes others from participation. The final factor is the social position of the individual; age, sex, race, religion, socioeconomic status, and so on fit into this category. Given limitations on data and methodology, and the purpose of his book, Milbrath does not seek to determine the relative importance of these factors.

Now, however, researchers have a better idea of the relative importance of various influences on political participation. One major theory, the resource model, was developed by Brady, Verba, and Schlozman (1995). This model stresses the importance of politically active people having resources in addition to interest: "... motivations such as interest in politics are not enough to explain political participation. The resources of time, money, and skills are also powerful predictors of political participation in America" (Brady et al., p. 285).

Resources include not only money but also skills derived from one's job or from holding organizational office in social organizations or churches. Another resource is large amounts of free time. The various types of political participation, such as voting, contributing funds, and working in political campaigns or attending protests, are dependent to different degrees on levels of free time, income, and number of civic skills (Brady et al., 1995). "To give a reductionist version of our findings—political interest is especially important for turnout; civic skills, for acts requiring an investment of time; and money, for acts involving an investment of money" (Brady et al., p. 285).

One variable, political interest, is important to understanding *all* of these types of political participation (Brady et al., 1995). Although level of education is an important predictor of political interest, a person's values are an important vehicle through which concern about current events can be molded into interest about politics. Remember, values are what allow political stimuli to reach an individual's consciousness and activate his or her behavior (Milbrath, 1965).

Given the nature of the social work profession, with relatively high levels of education (undergraduate or graduate degrees), high levels of civic skills (public speaking experience from classroom presentations, organizational skills from working in agencies, etc.), but not especially high incomes, we might wonder about the extent of social workers' involvement in the political process. The next section describes to what extent social workers, as a group, are politically active.

ARE SOCIAL WORKERS POLITICALLY ACTIVE?

Considerable literature on the role of social workers in politics exists, with the contributions generally falling into one of two camps. Either the contribution is a description of the "how to" of being active in politics (Albert, 1983; Ginsberg, 1988; Haynes & Mickelson, 2000; Mahaffey & Hanks, 1982; Patti & Dear, 1981; Richan, 1996; Salcido, 1984) or it examines whether or not social workers are politically involved (Amidei, 1987; Cohen, 1966; Ezell, 1993; Mary, Ellano, & Newell, 1993; Mathews, 1982; Pawlak & Flynn, 1990; Wolk, 1981).

The second of these categories is further divided into two types of writings. The first is exhortations directed at social workers to either increase their political efforts or to continue with the good things they are already doing (Amidei, 1987; Cohen, 1966). These articles usually have little empirical basis, other than some appropriate anecdotes.

The second type is a look at actual behavior. Some empirical work has been conducted to answer the question of how active social workers are in politics (Ezell, 1993; Mary et al., 1993; Mathews, 1982; Pawlak & Flynn, 1990; Wolk, 1981). Data indicate that National

Association of Social Work (NASW) members are more likely than the general population to report a party affiliation, with 74 percent associated with the Democratic party. Much smaller numbers of social workers said that they are Republicans (12 percent) or independent of any party affiliation (12 percent). A few (2 percent) were connected with other parties (NASW, 1995). These percentages are quite different than those for the entire American population. According to unpublished Gallup poll data from nearly the same time as the NASW survey, the American population was 32 percent Democratic, 36 percent independent of party affiliation, and 32 percent Republican (Stanley & Niemi, 1995, p.149). The NASW (p. 1) survey confirms other research which indicates that "social workers tend to be more politically active than the general population."

Earlier studies of political participation documented a similar story. "Social workers *are* political members of society" (Wolk, 1981, p. 287). Social workers, according to Wolk's data, are as active as members of other professions and business executives. Ezell (1993, p. 92), in a study somewhat comparable to Wolk's, finds that there was "significant growth in the political involvement of social workers" between 1981 and 1989. More specifically, Ezell (1993, p. 92) shows how social workers are active:

> . . . social workers are politically active largely by writing letters to public officials but also by discussing political issues with friends, by belonging to politically active organizations, and by attending political meetings. In addition, substantial proportions of social workers make campaign contributions and get involved in candidate elections.

More than other authors, Ezell (1993) also examines why the social workers in his study were active. "The major reasons social workers are involved in advocacy are because of personal values, professional responsibility, and they like to see things change" (Ezell, 1993, p. 89).

To summarize the chapter so far, research indicates that certain personal values contribute to both a sense of professional responsibility to engage in and a higher level of interest in engaging in advocacy. Educational level also affects the amount of interest in and skills needed for advocacy that a person possesses. Educational level also has a direct impact on the amount of advocacy, micro or macro, in which a person will engage. Participation in other organizations affects a person's skill level and also has a direct impact on advocacy because it provides additional opportunities to become an advocate. Finally, there must be time available to conduct advocacy. The relationships between these factors are shown in figure 3.1.

FIGURE 3.1   Factors leading to greater use of advocacy practice.

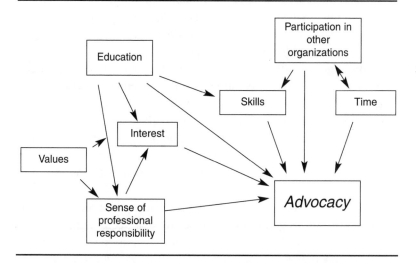

INFLUENCING THE FACTORS THAT LEAD TO GETTING INVOLVED

Knowing the factors that influence participation and advocacy is important, because it presents a systematic way to analyze incentives and barriers to getting involved, both personally and when recruiting others to become more active in advocacy. The next several sections address each factor in figure 3.1 and present concrete steps to "getting involved."

Education

Research indicates that people with higher levels of education tend to be more involved in political issues (Verba, Schlozman, & Brady, 1995). In the United States, higher education is strongly correlated with higher income. People with higher incomes tend to be active politically both because they can afford to do so and because they have more at stake in the system. Even in social work, higher education leads to higher income. So it is likely that higher levels of education also lead to higher levels of advocacy for social workers. Another reason that higher education may lead to higher levels of advocacy in the political world is that people with more education are more likely to become the executive directors of agencies and programs. Being in such a position requires a person to spend more time developing expertise to promote one's agency and to advocate in a macro arena for funding and on behalf of program clients (Ezell, 1991).

Although educational level is important in and of itself because of its impact on the ability to learn and analyze situations critically, and because of its correlation with income, the content of one's education is certainly important as well. A social work degree should lead to greater use of advocacy than, say, a degree in German. A social work education involves learning skills that are vital to advocacy practice and also should spark an interest in advocacy at both the case and cause levels.

There are several ways to affect a person's education level. Social work education programs are required by their accrediting body, the Council on Social Work Education, to include information on policy making and other forms of advocacy. If a program does not provide such information to students, there is cause for concern. Social work students should know that such information is required and should make plans to advocate within their school so that they can be prepared to skillfully use advocacy in their professional lives.

Agencies interested in higher levels of advocacy practice in their organization may want to increase the minimum level of social work education for the workers they hire and support the further education of non-MSW level social work staff already employed. Having staff with higher levels of education should increase the amount of advocating, all other things being equal.

Social workers are also involved in continuing education or professional development efforts and can learn more about advocacy through in-service training, conference presentations, and other learning opportunities. It is helpful for agency trainers, conference organizers, and professional development course providers to plan for education in advocacy practice.

Values

Personal values are the touchstone for most of the actions people take, including when they decide whether or not to use advocacy practice skills in a particular situation. Organizational values can also affect the amount of advocacy workers conduct. Values related to working for social justice include a strong sense of fairness, feeling that people should try to make a difference in the world, and, often, a religious background that emphasizes the equality and importance of all persons.

It is common to hear that the world is not fair, and so we should stop complaining. Adults tell children this in order to justify decisions and situations that are not fair and to ease the anger and hurt children feel when they or others are treated unfairly. The end result, after many repetitions, may be to blunt any desire to make the world more fair. After all, if the world is not fair now, and never has been, what sense does it make to try to change it now?

People who maintain their "childish" insistence that the world should be fair are likely to want to make a difference, whether they are social workers or not. Feeling angry at unfairness is often the precipitating factor for involvement.

Wanting the world to be fairer and actually deciding to try to do something about it can be separate issues. Sometimes people are overwhelmed with their situation and believe that they cannot reach out or extend themselves any further in order to promote social justice. Without feeling that they should try to make a difference, there is little impetus to take the extra steps required to get involved in advocacy.

The modern profession of social work is secular in nature, and most current aspects of social work training and education are nonreligious. Despite this fact, social work has religious roots, and many people who are outspoken social justice advocates for various populations are so because of their religious convictions. Not all religious backgrounds are equal in terms of their impact on advocacy, but most religions widely practiced in the United States are in agreement that people are created equally in the eyes of God and deserve equal opportunities.

Two principle paths exist for affecting the values of the workers in an organization: hiring people with the desired values and shaping and maintaining employees' values once they are hired. The first approach seems the easiest, but it is often difficult to know fully the values and ideas of an interviewee. Also, organizations have to choose from among the people who apply for a job, so it is not certain that the "perfect candidate" with the desired job skills, attitudes, and values will be hired in every case. Thus, it is vital for all social work organizations to have a plan in place to affect their employees' values.

An important way to accomplish this task is to pay close attention to the organizational culture. Every organization has a particular culture that is passed from worker to worker, sometimes consciously, more often though, unconsciously. Through this culture, workers come to learn the unwritten rules of the organization, which may or may not include an emphasis on advocating for clients. If an honest appraisal of the organization shows that front-line and other workers do not feel that advocacy is expected of them or that they can get in "a heap of trouble" for their advocacy efforts, it may be that the organization's culture is getting in the way of a more active focus on using advocacy.

In order to change culture in an organization, the leaders would have to make it clear that they expect and support professional advocacy efforts on the part of workers for their clients. Despite a strong willingness on the part of agency leaders, it is important to realize that culture change is a long and difficult process. In order to achieve a shift in organizational culture, the top leaders of the organization must alter what they pay attention to and measure, model the new behaviors, and rework the criteria they use to allocate rewards and status (Schein, 1997).

Sense of Professional Responsibility

Values, as discussed above, are very influential in whether or not a social worker decides to act as an advocate. Specifically, values affect and to some extent determine a person's sense of professional responsibility. A person's educational level is also linked to his or her sense of professional responsibility. The more that a person has been involved in a social work education, the greater is the likelihood that coursework has impressed upon the student the idea that social workers are supposed to advocate on behalf of their clients. An examination of social work ethics is supposed to be present in all coursework, so more social work education should lead to a greater sense of professional responsibility.

Although many types of classes can be useful for human service workers, no education is better for a professional social work job than a social work education. Social work students are brought face-to-face with key professional subjects that are not covered in other educational programs. Of these, one of the most important is the NASW Code of Ethics. Social work students are exposed to this material in many different ways and settings so that the richness and vitality, as well as the ambiguities and weaknesses, of the Code are infused in the educational process. This immersion can have a large impact on a person's sense of responsibility.

Most states have requirements for licensed social workers to receive continuing education credits from attending workshops and seminars; some states, such as Texas, require that at least some of these credits are in the area of professional ethics. Thus, the best way to affect a person's sense of responsibility is to involve him or her in a thorough and ongoing social work education focused on what social workers should be doing, why they should be doing it, and how they should be doing it. One aspect of this education should emphasize the need for advocacy and the ethical and professional ways to conduct advocacy. The more that a person believes that advocacy is an integral part of a social worker's practice repertoire, the greater the amount of advocacy the person will engage in.

Interest

A person not interested in advocacy is less likely to engage in it. Interest in advocacy can be stimulated by one's set of values, education, and sense of professional responsibility. Interest in advocacy can also be increased by performing advocacy.

Values guide much, if not all, of what we do on the job and off. If our values encourage us to look out for others, to work for social justice, to struggle against unfair inequality, and so on, we tend to want to take action when we see our values being violated.

Education can affect interest as well. One of the important elements of professional social work education is to bring new ideas and information to students—including ideas and information about how laws and policies affect us all. As the saying goes in social work, "Policy affects practice, and practitioners affect policy." Many people have not learned how decisions of federal, state, and local politicians and appointed officials make a difference in the daily lives of social workers and clients. This lack of knowledge is why the Council on Social Work Education requires that social policy be taught in all schools of social work.

Professional responsibility can lead to interest as well. Often a topic or duty is considered uninteresting because a person does not know much about it. Seeing how processes operate and observing their effects can open one's mind to topics formerly thought of as boring. Also, if some task, such as advocating for clients, has to be done, it may begin to seem more interesting as the process unfolds, if only to prevent cognitive dissonance from setting in.

Examples of these processes abound among students and in-the-field social workers. One social worker found herself interested in the minute details of client eligibility determination after finding out that one of her clients had been turned down for a program despite meeting all the requirements. Another worker began to explore the intricacies of budget decision making at the county level when his program budget was threatened with a 20 percent reduction in funding. A school social worker decided that the process of assigning English-as-a-second-language (ESL) teachers was an important topic after seeing a Vietnamese immigrant kindergartner crying at school and being unable to find anyone in the school who could communicate in that child's language.

Interest in advocacy and particular issues can also be linked directly to one's self-interest. If an issue threatens one's family, livelihood, neighborhood, quality of life, church, or other cherished elements of living, the interest level in that issue shoots up immediately. As an example, I became very involved in planning and zoning issues, the hazards of underground gasoline storage containers, and the connection between convenience stores and crime when a developer proposed building a gasoline station/convenience store in my neighborhood. These were not issues that I had hitherto been interested in. I became enough of an expert, however, to present information to my city council and persuade at least one council member to vote against the zoning change because of safety issues.

Many people operate within a rather limited comfort zone made up of the daily tasks of helping one client at a time. Others, particularly those on an administrative level, may become disconnected from the recipients of services and forget that the reason for the agency is to promote client health, well-being, and quality of life. Advocacy can be such a powerful and life-changing experience that it can help move us beyond a small comfort zone. It can also remind us of the passion for improving the world and the condition of people in it that we had as we entered the profession. Thus, one of the key ways to promote an interest in advocacy is to model the behavior for others, so that they, too, can see how it works and notice the results of the many small but necessary steps in the process. Even when advocacy is unsuccessful, the process of trying is an important way to kindle additional efforts that may be successful.

Another way to increase interest in advocacy is to show how it is in the person's self-interest to be an advocate. Advocacy may be tied to recognition, promotion, pay raises, greater status, or other extrinsic rewards. Naturally, there are intrinsic rewards as well, connected to a person's value system, sense of professional responsibility, and other individual characteristics.

An important element to remember when beginning an advocacy effort is that it can be started and completed by one person. Working to help one client with rules that are hard to follow and are needlessly bureaucratic can be done without other people's involvement. Interest can be self-generated and then spread to others, as one candle can light another while still burning brightly itself.

Skills

One of the barriers to participating in advocacy practice is the sense that one does not have the skills needed to be effective. Social workers can see the need for increased services, greater funding, or more inclusive policy, yet still do little or nothing because they do not know what to do, who to see, or what can make a difference. This lack of skills may or may not be real, but the perception is what matters. This book, for example, is an effort to affect the level of skill that social workers have and the confidence they have in their skills.

The more educated a person is about advocacy—whether from classes in college or graduate school, from workshops at professional conferences, from having a mentor, or just from trial and error—the greater the likelihood that he or she will use advocacy in the future. Practice also is an important element in learning new skills, so an advocate's education should include ample opportunities to perform advocacy tasks.

Two elements are vital to increasing skills in advocacy, as in other areas of practice: education and experience. I addressed these elements earlier. A third aspect that can make a large difference is the presence of a mentor or guide. Having someone to learn from or to bounce ideas off of can be one of the best ways to improve one's skills quickly. Learning from books and other literature is another way to increase skills. Trial and error can also work, but is inefficient and can be more discouraging than necessary.

Agencies wanting to improve the advocacy skills of their staff can do so by making sure that experienced, competent advocates are already on staff and by providing them time to mentor and assist other workers with less well-developed skills. Having books and other literature in the agency library is helpful, as is keeping an up-to-date list of useful Web sites for both skills enhancement and substantive content purposes.

Participation in Other Organizations

An element of the acquisition of advocacy skills that is often overlooked is the level of participation in other (non-job) organizations. People who participate in organizations learn things about how organizations work in general. They also pick up skills from being in leadership or supportive positions in those organizations. Being active in a church is one particularly common example. The range of volunteer positions in churches is long, and each one contributes to a participant's knowledge about "how the world works." This knowledge and experience can often be applied to understanding advocacy and can make one feel comfortable when speaking out on an issue or on behalf of a client. Activity in other organizations also provides access to larger numbers of contacts, all of whom can be communicated with on behalf of an individual client or group of clients. A person can also learn how to influence policy making by seeing how others influence their organization's actions.

Much of the improvement in advocacy efforts related to increased participation comes from participation in organizations that are related to a person's private interests—an educational experience that comes "free of charge" because the person wants to attend a particular church, to be involved in a particular hobby or sport, or is interested in something such as the environment. These interests lead to organizational involvement and an increased understanding of the ways of the world.

An agency can foster a similar type of involvement by assigning or allowing employees to become active in coalitions that are working on issues, such as homelessness, child health, or emergency social services, and in professional organizations, such as the National Association of Social Workers, at the local, state, and/or national levels. Although "over involvement" in outside organizations can happen once in a while, usually such added exposure of the employee and her agency is helpful to the organization and worth the time away from normal work duties. Not only do more people in the field know this particular employee, but the exchange of information and skills across organizational boundaries can help the entire social services system, thus improving client outcomes. Having these types of connections is also a powerful asset when advocates can reach across agency walls for help with individual clients and policy issues.

Time

We would clearly expect people with more time to be able to advocate more. Time is, however, limited for everyone. Each of us has only twenty-four hours per day to sleep, eat, work, relax, and so on. How we allocate that time is the most important decision we make with our lives. And it is not always true that the people with the most free time are the most likely to be strong advocates. As the saying goes, "If you want something done, delegate it to a busy person." The ability to focus and to know what is important in our lives (what our values are, in other words) affect our perception of the availability of time for advocacy more than the actual amount of time in the day or the amount of time we work do.

The allocation of our twenty-four hours per day can greatly be affected by job design and job expectations. Job design is important because it affects workers' ability to use their time *productively*. Thus, even if all other aspects of life are equal, people with greater flexibility in their job schedules may be more likely to perform advocacy than a person who has less flexibility, if only because flexibility allows a reallocation of time that maximizes productivity in other job elements. For example, some people have more defined times to work than others. A traditional job might start at 8:00 a.m. and end at 5:00 p.m. Another person might have flextime, which entails working the same number of hours but at different times. For example, they can start earlier, say at 7:00 a.m. and end at 4:00 p.m. Another approach might be to work four days per week for ten hours each day. One way flexible work times could lead to greater use of advocacy is if a person who is able to function well early in the morning completes mandatory paperwork early in the day and thus has afternoon time (when decision makers may be more available and amenable to influence) for writing to, talking to, and visiting advocacy targets. Although flextime does not give a worker "more" time than another, job design can increase the amount of *productive* time.

Also, different jobs have different levels of advocacy practice associated with them. Although advocacy is a part of all social workers' jobs, administrators typically use more of their workday for advocacy than do direct service workers (Ezell, 1994). Thus, the expectations of the administrators' jobs are more conducive to allocating time to advocacy.

Although social work administrators are expected to devote time to macrolevel advocacy, job requirements and expectations also are important for direct service workers. If organization supervisors' spoken or unspoken message is that "advocacy for our clients is part of the job" and they incorporate the message into formal and informal job performance ratings, staff will consider advocacy practice to be more important and will increase their advocacy work.

CONCLUSION

This chapter has laid out the first step in the advocacy practice process, getting involved. It discussed two main issues: the reasons why people are active in politics and the variables that influence people to use advocacy. These topics are vital to understanding both why a particular person may be involved in advocacy and how to influence others to get involved. After reading this information, you may have gained insight into why you are, or perhaps why you are *not*, interested and active in politics. You may also have learned something about why you may or may not currently be interested in client advocacy at the case or cause level.

Many of the variables discussed are amenable to change—in you, in your colleagues, and even in clients. Education, values, and sense of professional responsibility are particularly important to stress in your own life and the lives of your social work colleagues. Learning about the other organizations that colleagues and clients participate in and the skills they have learned may allow you to discover people who are already involved and who may be excellent advocates and perhaps mentors for you.

Suggested Further Reading

Verba, S., Schlozman, K., & Brady, H. (1995). *Voice and equality: Civic voluntarism in American politics*. Cambridge, MA: Harvard University Press.

A modern classic of political science, these authors explore thoroughly how the American people make their voices heard in a democratic government. Based on surveys of and interviews with political activists and ordinary citizens, the authors develop and present a comprehensive model of political participation.

Chapter 4

UNDERSTANDING THE ISSUE

The small sign in the vacant lot was a bad omen. A local developer wanted to rezone the land to build a convenience store/gas station and strip mall right next to an older but well-maintained area of housing, which was across the street from a large park. The public hearing was in one week. The one person who had noticed the sign was walking the streets of the neighborhood, looking for signatures on a petition, and making calls for action—let's write the members of the city council, call the newspaper, picket the developer's office. We have to do something, and we have to do it now!

The person in the based-on-true-events vignette above is like many people are when first confronted with a situation that might call for advocacy. Once interest has been sparked, there is a desire to move to action. Time always seems short, and there is a natural desire not to allow a bad situation to continue any longer than necessary. Having an interest in the case or cause seems to instill potential advocates with an irresistible urge to get going and make a difference *right now*.

It is important to know that resistance to this urge is not futile— do not begin to take action just yet. Before *effective* action can begin, a potential advocate must understand the issue. This chapter provides a way of making sure that the issue is understood: who benefits, who loses, and why. Without understanding the issue, the advocate is likely to make many mistakes and waste much time in trying to assist clients. In this chapter, I also describe practical policy analysis tools.

Understanding usually comes in small stages, in which one piece of information fits into another and produces greater knowledge than either piece on its own does. Such synergy is the end goal of the advocacy research process. Research, in this sense, may be very sophisticated, using statistical analysis and a thorough library search of relevant literature. But usually it is not. Usually, advocacy research is directed at answering one, or a small number of, questions, because it is believed that these answers will have an affect on decision makers. This process can be broken into five steps, as shown in figure 4.1.

FIGURE 4.1   Steps to Understanding the Issue

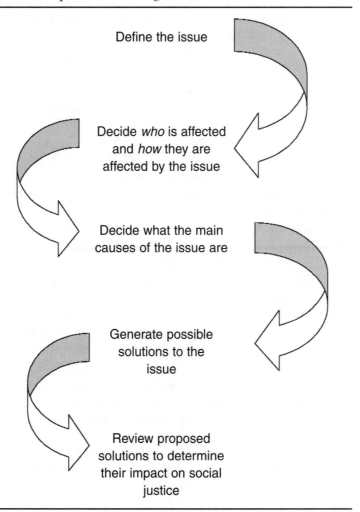

Define the issue

Decide *who* is affected and *how* they are affected by the issue

Decide what the main causes of the issue are

Generate possible solutions to the issue

Review proposed solutions to determine their impact on social justice

STEP 1: DEFINE THE ISSUE

An often overlooked step is defining the issue, as unambiguously as possible. Without being able to specify what the issue is, it will be impossible to understand it. Having a few facts at hand does not constitute a definition of an issue. A definition is important, because "the same facts . . . are often interpreted in markedly different ways. . . . Hence, the same policy-relevant information can and often does result in conflicting definitions and explanations of a 'problem'" (Dunn, 1981, p. 97). It is also important to understand the difference between a "problem" and a "condition"—a condition is defined as a problem only when we decide something should be done about it (Kingdon, 1995, p. 109). Definitions are often shaped, to a very large extent, by the values of the person doing the defining. These values are the lens through which the issue is categorized.

The way an issue is categorized has important implications for how it will be solved. For example, not too many years ago, if a client came to a social worker with the presenting problem of being hit by her spouse, the issue would probably have been seen as a medical problem (if the physical harm was severe) and perhaps also as need for marital counseling. It is far more likely nowadays that the social worker would see this as an issue of domestic violence and bring law enforcement officials into the picture to force the batterer to change, perhaps by receiving anger management training. Referral to a local domestic violence shelter would also almost certainly be made, if available. Thus, the issue is now being defined as a social problem more than an individual problem and the batterer's problem more than the victim's problem.

In another example of the importance of defining the issue, Kingdon (1995) describes the situation of transportation for people with handicaps as being a battle over the proper definition of the issue. If it is defined as a transportation issue, appropriate solutions are to provide subsidized taxi rides or dial-a-ride services. These services provide relatively inexpensive and convenient ways to get to places, thus people with handicaps avoid being isolated from the rest of society. On the other hand, if the situation is defined as a civil rights issue, where separate accommodations are not equal, then proper solutions are to make public transportation accessible by installing elevators, lifts in buses, curb cuts for wheelchairs, and so on. In clinical work, this process may be called "framing" the client's issue. Just as with clinical work, sometimes the role of the social worker is to "reframe" the issue, if the current framing approach is not leading to successful intervention.

Problem Setting

Because the generalist model of social work is a rational, problem-solving approach to changing the world, we must deal with the topic of goal setting. But before we can set a goal (a process that we will examine in chap. 5), we must clearly set forth the problem. In some jobs, it is possible to envision a better future without reference to what is broken or untenable about today. But in social work, we work with clients who experience hunger, psychic pain, and mental illness and encounter situations of deprivation, discrimination, and desperation every day. Because we see so many problems, we cannot retreat to an ivory tower of perfection. Due to the many issues that we may attend to in our work, whether with one person or a community, it becomes vital to find a single problem to work on for each advocacy effort. This one problem may have many facets and several subsidiary problems, but we must find a way to encapsulate the issues into one problem statement. We do this in order to attain a focus for ourselves, our clients, decision makers, and others, such as potential allies or enemies who may be interested.

A problem can be defined as a situation that should be changed and can be changed. Thus, biologically based situations such as being left-handed cannot be defined as a problem because it cannot really be changed. A teacher's reaction to left-handed students may be a problem, however, as she may want to force the children to learn to write with their right hands. This may be a situation that should be changed because research shows that children who prefer their left hands for writing can be damaged academically if they are not allowed to develop their preference. And, we believe, the teacher may be open to changing her beliefs and behavior if she can be reached through advocacy by a school social worker. Thus, we can define the problem as the teacher's reaction to the situation, rather than as the left-handedness itself, which is merely a situation.

Practice looking at the world with this definition of a problem. You will quickly realize that many situations commonly called problems are not actually problems. It is not that these situations should not be changed, but rather that you feel they cannot or will not be changed. When encountering such a situation, the advocate's sense of social justice must take over and help him or her to find the part of the situation that can be changed. It is also possible to use reframing to keep the situation from leading to burnout. The following story about a girl and starfish illustrates this purpose for reframing:

> One bright morning a girl and her dad were walking along the beach near their home. Overnight, some freak occurrence of nature had stranded thousands of starfish on the beach. The girl was walking along, picking up as many of the dying creatures as possible, one by one, throwing them back to the salty, life-giving water. The dad praised his daughter for her efforts, but told her that she couldn't really make a significant impact on the overall situation. The girl looked thoughtfully at her father and said, "Dad, you may be right. But it makes a big difference to the ones I throw back!" (adapted from Eiseley, 1979)

No advocate can bring social justice to everyone. But by working carefully with their clients and others, advocates can make a big difference to the ones they do reach. You do not have to define the problem as thousands of people who lack food, are poorly housed, or are in danger of violence to be an advocate. You can define the problem as *this* man is hungry, *this* family's home is falling down, *this* child is in danger of being hit. Your efforts can make a world of difference to those individuals.

There are three possible approaches to problem (or issue, as we are using the term) definition: accepting the client's definition of the problem, using a pragmatic approach, and using the social-criterion approach (Patton & Sawicki, 1993).

Accepting the client's definition is an approach barely mentioned in Patton and Sawicki's (1993) policy analysis text, yet it is very important in the field of social work. It is part of the social work ethos of "starting where the client is." If a client indicates that she is having trouble getting her unemployment check and as a result is facing eviction, the social worker needs to look carefully at the issue the client is presenting for a solution. It may be that there is an underlying issue, such as the client not following through with paperwork or the client using rent money for other purposes, but the proper thing for a social work advocate to do may be to simply accept the client's definition as a starting point until he or she can collect additional information.

It can be fairly easy to get the client's view of the problem when working with clients in individual-level advocacy. The client can be considered as the "problem expert." What systemic barriers are getting in the way? What feelings are causing difficulty? What resources are lacking that would ease the situation? The client may be able to answer these questions readily. Significant others in the client's life may be able to provide additional, even if at times contradictory, insights into and views of the problem.

Social workers, with their training and professional expertise, also have much to contribute to the problem-setting process. It is possible that the client believes that society is to blame for his lack of success, when, to the social worker, this may be only part of the problem. Conversely, the client may want to take on full responsibility for a negative situation that can truly only be fully resolved at a community level. In either case, the analytical perspectives and techniques the social worker has learned can be of great value in helping the client focus and thus be able to move quickly from here to there.

The process of problem setting is similar for a larger aggregation of people, such as an organization, a community group, or society, except that as the number of people increases, the chances of getting complete agreement on what *the* problem is diminishes rapidly. Still, the social worker's task in these circumstances is to work with a smaller group that can speak for the others. The task is then to get as much of a consensus as possible with this representative group.

A drawback in accepting a client definition is that the client might view the issue differently than the professional social worker does, as was briefly mentioned above. For example, the client might view her issue as an individual failure when you believe it is the result of more systemic processes. Not being able to find a job in an area marked by high unemployment is one such situation. Alternatively, the client may want to blame others when you believe that the client can do something to fix the problem on an individual basis. An example of this might be that the client is not trying to stop using illegal drugs, saying that he is genetically predisposed to addiction. In both cases, the best approach, in the short run, may be to work toward a synthesis of the client's view and the social worker's view.

Another concern with using the client's definition of the problem is that it may be unclear who the client is, particularly with a macro-level situation. In the case described at the beginning of this chapter, a community worker might immediately want to deny the zoning change request to prevent the construction of a convenience store/gas station and strip mall across the street from a large park and next to an established neighborhood. But it may be that some people living in the area would like to have such a close place to buy gas, and people who frequent the park might like to be able to buy cold drinks or ice on a hot day. Is the client the person who is leading the fight against the zoning change, the neighborhood as a whole (including both those who might be in favor and those who might be against it), or the city as a whole? Although the answer probably depends on who employs the potential advocate, the question must be answered if one is to take the client's definition of the problem.

The pragmatic approach. If taking this approach, an advocate would be interested in understanding an issue only when there is disagreement about how the issue should be handled and when there are other ways to handle the problem than the one currently being used. In other words, if everyone agrees that there is nothing that can be done to change the situation or no one has a better idea, the pragmatically minded advocate would look for some other client to assist or some other issue to work on.

The danger of a pragmatic approach is that the social worker may become too cynical to seize the opportunities for change that exist, given the right approach. It is easy to say, even metaphorically, "You can't fight city hall" to indicate that nothing can be done to alter the situation, whether one is dealing with an individual or community issue. Often, however, more change can be made to happen than a quick look at the situation would suggest. It might take more than the usual amount of effort, but creative solutions can emerge that increase the range of options that can be implemented.

Social criterion approach. An advocate using the social-criterion approach actively searches for issues and tries to define issues that should be solved. This approach involves an intricate calculation of whether an issue is an individual problem or a societal problem that requires intervention from others. The advocate usually chooses to work on problems that are both *widespread* (that is, affecting large numbers of people) and *serious* (that is, causing considerable distress to people who experience the problem). However, widespread problems may not be defined as serious problems, and serious problems may not be widespread enough for social intervention (Patton & Sawicki, 1993). If either is the case, that particular problem will be less likely to have an advocate trying to solve it.

Two dangers are associated with using the social-criterion approach. First, the potential advocate may wrongly place the issue on the individual-societal continuum. This placement of the issue entails defining the situation in such a way as to place blame on individuals for problems caused or exacerbated by social forces or institutions. This placement could also entail deciding that the cause of a situation was social in nature when it could, in fact, be fixed by the individuals experiencing the issue. Another danger of the social-criterion approach is that it may consume too much time in trying to be very inclusive of all issues in a community. It is also unrealistic to expect employees of agencies to be on the constant lookout for new issues to emerge—they generally have more than enough issues already vying for their attention.

An example may clarify the different approaches to defining an issue. The activist mentioned at the start of this chapter is concerned about a convenience store/gas station with an accompanying strip mall being built in his neighborhood. Using a client viewpoint–acceptance approach, a social worker in the city's community development office brought in for advice would just accept that building a convenience store/gas station and strip mall is a problem or may lead to a number of problems. Another social worker, using the pragmatic approach, might look at what else could be proposed for the land and how successful a challenge to the new zoning would be before deciding on a definition of the issue. If the zoning board and city council have already decided to support the proposal, the social worker advocate might decide to look for another way to use his or her time. However, if some disagreement exists among the members of the decision-making body, he or she would look at other ways to approach the use of that land. The social worker understands that how an issue is defined has an impact on how the issue is perceived and thus on which solution may be chosen. Finally, the social-criterion approach social worker would be out in the field on a regular basis, trying to find out what is going on in the community. This social worker might have in his or her head to be looking at vacant land and monitoring closely the rezoning applications that are turned in, believing that vigilance is needed to look proactively at land use decisions, particularly those that bring in low-end retail shopping. He will maintain ties with many people, always searching for land-use solutions that improve the distribution of life chances for residents of the neighborhood.

A good problem definition will put some parameters around the situation. It will describe a gap between what should be (based on a vision of social justice) and the reality facing the social worker. It will be specific and, in and of itself, a call to action. The following are sample problem statements:

> Children are going to bed hungry in our city.
>
> I have a client who is being denied a bank loan for home improvements because her neighborhood is redlined.
>
> Elementary school children in the local school district who speak only Vietnamese do not have access to anyone at school who speaks their language.
>
> Minority youth in our community are being arrested more often and getting longer sentences than white kids are for the same offences.

Keep in mind that as you move through the steps of understanding an issue, you may find that you want to change your definition of the issue. This change is acceptable, as it shows you have learned something important. A compelling definition of the issue is a necessary part of understanding an issue, but more information is needed before moving ahead to doing something.

STEP 2: DECIDE WHO IS AFFECTED AND HOW THEY ARE AFFECTED

The second step to understanding the issue is to look at who is affected, both positively and negatively. Although it may seem odd to think about who benefits from a problem, this perspective helps us remember that laws, rules, conditions, and "the way things are" do not occur by chance. If negative situations occurred by chance, then the situations would most likely be altered quickly.

Depending on how you have defined the issue in the first step, you may be considering this as an issue affecting only one person or many. Let's take an example from the list provided earlier and say that we have a client who is unable to get a bank loan for home improvements. The client indicates that she filed all the requested paperwork and has adequate income to repay the loan. Due to confidentiality requirements, the bank officials that the social worker has contacted for information are unwilling to talk without the client present. The social worker suspects that the client's neighborhood has been redlined, that is, banks have decided not to give loans to anyone who wants to improve property located in a certain area. The social worker and potential advocate asks the following question: Who is (or may be) affected by this situation and how?

A quickly made list of answers to this question includes the following:

1. The client who didn't get the loan is negatively affected by a deteriorating physical environment.
2. Everyone else living in the neighborhood is negatively affected by a deteriorating physical environment.
3. Neighborhood institutions such as businesses, churches, etc., are negatively affected by a deteriorating physical environment.

4. The bank or banks involved (as institutions) are, currently, positively affected, as they have no risk of default if they do not make loans to people in a low-income neighborhood. In the future, they may be affected negatively, as redlining (if that is what is happening) is not a legal practice. Even if the case is not proven in court, the bank or banks will suffer negative publicity if the charges are made public.

5. The bankers making loan decisions (as individuals) are, currently, probably positively affected, as their job security may depend on keeping profits high. In the future, if this situation is brought to court and proven, this could have very negative effects on these individuals, including fines and/or jail terms.

6. Developers and landlords may be positively affected, as the value of homes that are not well-maintained deteriorates and thus may be less expensive for developers and landlords of low-rent housing to purchase.

7. Businesses that supply home fix-up materials are negatively affected, as people wanting to fix up a deteriorating physical environment are denied funds, which prevents them from buying supplies at these businesses.

8. The community as a whole is, currently, negatively affected, due to a physically deteriorating area of town. Such areas tend to sink further, bringing additional crime and violence to that part of town, which requires additional police resources. There may be a small current positive effect if the money that might be loaned to fix up deteriorating homes in one part of the city is used on other more economically profitable projects.

9. Banking regulatory officials, if redlining is occurring by the bank, are possibly negatively affected, as they may have to conduct an investigation.

10. Law enforcement officials, if a crime has been committed, are possibly negatively affected, as they may have to conduct an investigation.

Just this short list shows that many people and institutions are (or may be) affected, some negatively, some positively, while some, such as the community as a whole, may have some negative and some positive consequences. Laying out who is or may be affected and how they are affected allows the advocate to think about potential allies (those who might be willing to try to change the current situation) and potential challengers (those trying to maintain the current situation).

Alternative and/or additional ways of determining who is affected and how vary in their level of sophistication. These are four "back of the envelope" ways to determine the size of the population affected: *guess* the number, get *experts* to help you guess the number, look up the number in a *reference source*, and collect the number through a *systematic survey* or other investigation (Mosteller, 1977, pp. 163-164).

Each of these methods has advantages and disadvantages as a way of understanding the scope of the issue. The advantage of the guess is its ease of application. Anyone can come up with a guess, educated or not, about the scope of an issue. All guesses should be defensible, based on other techniques, such as extrapolation and projection, but often they are not. Advocates for a particular issue are often accused of "lying with statistics" about the size of a problem. For example, guesses at the size of the homeless population differ by several hundred percent—often the size of the guess is related to the purpose of the guess. People who want more funding for programs to assist the homeless favor a broad definition of homelessness, which results in a large number of people being counted as eligible for categorization as homeless. Government officials, or others who wish to minimize the size of the homeless population, move from the opposite position, finding that homelessness is less of an issue because of a stricter definition of what homelessness is. Without knowing the exact genesis of a social statistic, a potential user should approach it with caution (Best, 2001).

Many of the same caveats apply to the use of experts in the guessing process. Experts, by definition, know something about the issue in question, but experts are almost never neutral and may have ties to particular value stances that affect their estimates of the scope of an issue.

Many issues will not have accurate counts of the numbers of people affected, particularly in a small area. But one should not automatically assume this is true. Census Bureau data can be broken down into quite small areas called census tracts, so many local needs assessments can provide useful and accurate information that has already been collected. City and county planning departments and United Way, or other private planning bodies, often sponsor surveys of various topics.

Systematic surveys or other research are the best way to have an accurate understanding of how many people and organizations are involved in an issue, and if open-ended questions are included, very clear insights into how people and organizations are affected can be made. The disadvantages of this approach are its costs, difficulty, and need for expertise to have a truly valid and reliable survey.

STEP 3: DECIDE THE MAIN CAUSES OF THE ISSUE

In any situation, one can identify proximate (or immediate) causes, even if it is difficult to locate "true" (or ultimate) causes of social issues. A search for ultimate causes generally ends up in a dispute over values and religious or philosophic views. For example, we may be able to trace many of the current problems of poverty to a history of an economically stratified and racist social structure in the United States, but what caused such a social structure? A selfish human nature might be called the ultimate cause, but what is the cause of that nature? At some point, then, it becomes useless to argue causes, particularly ultimate causes. Still, an understanding of proximate causes must be attempted.

Different definitions of the issue lead to different ideas about the proximate cause. For example, after interviewing our client who didn't get a home improvement loan and the bank employee who processed the loan, we might find out that the client was not sure what all the terms on the application meant and did not have all the requested supporting documents. In this case, we might identify the proximate cause of the loan not being approved as problems with the application due to the lack of knowledge and preparation of the applicant. On the other hand, we might suspect that the employee working on the loan application was not as helpful as possible and was looking for an excuse to turn down the application. Without additional information, we cannot really say what the cause of the issue is.

At this point, our definition of the problem and the analysis of who is affected and how is useful. If we have determined that only a few people have had their applications denied and that all had problems understanding the application form, our interpretation of the issue's cause would most likely be a lack of individual knowledge. If we have determined that more than a few people from different areas of town have been turned down and that they all report uncaring bank employees, we can believe that the cause of the issue has something to do with the selection and training of the bank staff. If we have found that many people living in one geographic area have had their applications turned down, we are more likely to believe that the bank is using a set of systematic and discriminatory guidelines. Once we have decided what is causing the problem, we are ready to devise ways of solving it.

STEP 4: GENERATE POSSIBLE SOLUTIONS TO THE ISSUE

One of the most difficult, yet most interesting, aspects of the advocacy process is generating possible solutions. It is difficult in that after one or two solutions come to mind quickly, more creative options seem hard to generate. It is interesting, however, in that the ability to devise novel solutions is rewarding to the advocate if the solutions are adopted as a "better idea" than current practice.

Although the phrase *think outside the box* has become so overused that it may be considered trite, solutions should be developed that are not bound by currently perceived boundaries or structures. Four approaches to developing solutions are described next.

Brainstorming

Although the following approaches can be completed by one person, it is often useful to proceed with at least a small group in a brainstorming session. Brainstorming is a process of generating ideas without evaluating them along the way. It can be used as its own technique but is also often an integral part of other methods of idea generation as well. Because the term *brainstorming* is so common, most people have heard of it and even participated in what have been called brainstorming sessions. Still, a review of the basic principles of a brain-storming session is important, if only because they are often violated by untrained facilitators:

1. Have a leader and a recorder (though one person may fulfill both roles).
2. Clearly define what the brainstorming is about—everyone involved should be working on the same issue.
3. Have rules to guide the process. The following are common rules: everyone is allowed to participate, comments about the ideas generated (if any) should be nonjudgmental, all ideas should be recorded unless they are a repeat of an earlier idea, and a time limit should be set and adhered to.
4. If ideas seem lacking, sterile, or obvious, the leader can introduce "random" words to stimulate creativity. These words are best if they come from outside the main topic area and if they are tangible nouns rather than abstract ideas. The idea behind the use of random words is to spark creativity by injecting unusual images or ideas into the mix.
5. Evaluate the responses after the time limit for generating ideas is up. Evaluation includes grouping similar ideas, eliminating responses that do not apply or fit, and discussing the plusses and minuses of the remaining ideas as a group. (Osborn, 1963)

The "George Costanza" Approach

This approach is named in honor of a fictional character on the television show *Seinfeld*. In one episode, George decides that his usual approach to dating and life in general is not having the desired effect. He therefore decides to consider what he would usually do, then do the opposite. In the episode, George immediately begins to experience success in every aspect of his life. To apply this approach in your work, think of the typical response by the client, worker, and/or agency. Given that there is a problem based on this typical response, what would the opposite response be? Is there more than one "opposite" response? What would they be?

The "Win-Win" or "Super-Optimizing" Approach

This approach is based on the work of Stuart Nagel (2002), a prominent policy analysis scholar, and is outlined in his *Handbook of Public Policy Evaluation*. The basic idea of Nagel's win-win approach is to create an alternative policy that restructures the current situation to make it both more equitable and more efficient. Nagel outlines a number of basic approaches that have been successful (see table 4.1). Using this checklist, a social work advocate can develop alternative solutions for further consideration, whether the issue at hand is at a micro-, mezzo-, or macrolevel. By starting off saying, "What would happen if we ... " and then adding each phrase in table 4.1, many ideas can be created that might not have been thought of without this set of prompts.

The "What Can Be Done?" Approach

An additional way to generate solutions to an issue is the "What Can Be Done?" approach, loosely based on the feasible-manipulations

TABLE 4.1   Developing Win-Win Policy Alternatives

1. expand the resources
2. find a third party benefactor
3. set higher goals
4. minimize the causes of the problem
5. redefine the problem to emphasize goals rather than alternatives
6. increase the benefits and decrease the costs
7. socialize children in widely accepted values so the problem does not occur
8. find a new technology
9. contract out via an auction to multiple firms with societal strings attached
10. promote international economic communities
11. arrange for major benefits on one side and small costs on the other
12. fully combine alternatives that are not mutually exclusive
13. develop a multifaceted package
14. adopt the win-win solution in steps, in which the first step may be a traditional compromise

Reprinted from Nagel, S. (2002). *Handbook of Public Policy Evaluation* (p. 6). Thousand Oaks, CA: Sage.

approach developed by May (1981). The focus of the "What Can Be Done?" approach is to look at important variables in the issue and develop alternatives that fall on a continuum of "easily done" to "done only with difficulty." The first step in the process is to determine what elements of the situation are changeable, that is, what about the situation or its causes *can* be changed and what *should* be changed. These are written in the left-hand column of a table, one variable in each row. The analyst should also determine different actions that can be taken with regard to each variable; these actions should range from changes that are relatively *easy* to make to changes that are relatively *difficult* to make.

As an example, we'll look at the issue of bank loans being denied, as we have earlier in the chapter. Each of the identified variables—applicant knowledge, bank employee selection, bank employee training, and possible bank discriminatory practices—has been examined. In table 4.2, for each variable at least one possible action that is relatively easy to do, one that is moderately easy to do, and one that is relatively difficult to do has been described. The advocate, at this point, has a number of options from which to choose, any of which should improve the situation to some extent.

No matter which approach you use to generate alternative solutions (and it may be very useful to use more than one technique), you can evaluate the possible actions on the basis of their anticipated effect on social justice.

STEP 5: REVIEW PROPOSED SOLUTIONS' IMPACT ON SOCIAL JUSTICE

The fifth step is to review the various solutions that are proposed and to determine how likely they are to lead to social justice. The basic approach to creating and looking at possible solutions is to ask, repeatedly, What would be the results of adopting this solution? Who would be assisted? Who would be harmed? How would this solution act upon people currently affected negatively by this issue? How would this solution act upon people currently affected positively by this issue? Proposed solutions leading to greater social justice should be ranked higher in preference than solutions that do not improve social justice

TABLE 4.2   "What Can Be Done?" Approach Example:
Turned-Down Bank Loans

| Variable | Ease of Doing | | |
	Relatively Easy to Do	Moderately Easy to Do	Relatively Difficult to Do
Applicant Knowledge	Develop materials to explain the loan process for in-person or Web exchange	Change when information can be transmitted via in-person classes; improve computer access to information on the Web	Increase applicants' free time to learn about home buying or the loan process
Bank Employee Selection	Increase/change places where loan application processor positions are advertised	Expand applicant pool to include more people of color and other minorities	Alter job requirements for loan application processor job
Bank Employee Training	Introduce basic "soft" skills into the training, such as a customer service philosophy	Provide/mandate ethnic and cultural sensitivity training	Change current procedures for becoming a loan application processor to require that most "hard" job skills (use of computers, ability to compute numbers, etc.) are already known
Possible Discriminatory Bank Practices	File complaint with banking regulatory bodies	File EEO case	File criminal case

as much. This part of the chapter examines a few quick ways to evaluate alternative solutions to the issue.

Six Thinking Hats

One approach to evaluating possible solutions is the "Six Thinking Hats" approach (De Bono, 1999). The basic principle underlying this approach is that there is more than one thinking style. Each can contribute to a balanced evaluation of a proposed solution. Some of the conflict that arises in group discussions emanates from people using these different thinking styles. By rotating among all six styles and having everyone use the same thinking style at once, all styles are given their proper due and better decisions can be made. This approach also works with just one person, who also rotates among the six styles, thereby moving beyond his or her usual and dominant thinking style. When combined with a clear focus on the goal of achieving greater social justice, use of the six thinking hats approach has the potential to improve the quality of the decision process and the development of more easily implemented and workable plans. I discuss the six hats (or thinking styles) next.

The **white hat** is the rational style, as data analysis and historical interpolation are the key methods of understanding. Gaps in the data are identified, as are ways around those gaps.

The **red hat** is the intuitive style, as emotion, subjectivity, and gut reactions are the key methods of understanding the situation. Trying to understand other people's emotional and gut reactions, not just one's own, is an important element in this style. With this hat, the social worker should ask how people will react to the decision made, especially if they do not know the reasons behind it.

The **black hat** is the "negative" style, as the negatives of the situation or proposed solution are brought out. The following questions should be asked: What are the weaknesses of the proposal? How can it be shot down? What might go wrong? Can those possibilities be lessened? By systematically focusing on problems with the potential solution, the decision is made stronger.

By having everyone adopt the "naysayer" role, potential problems are brought into the open without anyone being unfairly labeled as unduly pessimistic. This protects lower status group members from higher status group members who might take criticism of their ideas personally.

The **yellow hat** is the "optimistic" style, as the emphasis is on the possible benefits of the proposal and the value of the idea. When the proposal is in trouble or having difficulties, the ideas generated in the yellow hat stage are invaluable for keeping momentum going.

The **green hat** is the "creative" style, as the emphasis is on seeing the situation in different ways. Techniques such as brainstorming, random word seeding, use of analogies or similes, and so on, can be used to see things in a different way.

The **blue hat** is the conductor's hat, as the outcome of this type of thinking is to decide how the decision process for the meeting should be structured. A blue hat period is often at the beginning of a gathering, when the agenda is set, rules for the meeting are proposed and agreed to by participants, and other decisions are made about how to proceed. Unlike using the other hats, one person, usually the group leader or meeting facilitator, keeps the blue hat on during the entire process. Others may also put on this hat to assist moving the discussion along, such as noting that someone is using the wrong hat for this point in the meeting. Blue hat thinking also summarizes discussions, provides overviews, and states conclusions. This can occur during the meeting as well as at its end.

"Putting on" one hat after another encourages a thorough examination of any proposed solution and, combined with a focus on social justice, may greatly improve the preliminary solution. This approach is also useful when comparing multiple possible solutions in that this multifaceted look at the different solutions to the same issue will bring out each alternative's strengths and weaknesses.

Social Justice Scorecard

Many different variations of a scorecard approach exist (see, for example, the description of approaches in Patton & Sawicki, 1993, pp. 349-355). The basic idea, however, is to compare alternatives without being able to reduce their characteristics to one number or score. Because the primary criterion for choosing a solution is to determine which solution most achieves social justice, the Social Justice Scorecard has been developed, using four attributes of social justice from a social work perspective based on Abbott's (1988) work (see chap. 2). Each alternative strategy is listed in a separate column and can be graded or ranked in relation to each of the social justice attributes. These rankings can be made in either an absolute way (as shown in table 4.3) or in a relative way (worst, medium, best), using either numbers or a qualitative ordinal scale such as is shown. The Social Justice

Scorecard should include a "do nothing" option among the alternative strategies to make clear the rankings for maintaining the status quo. Separate scorecards can be developed from different perspectives as well, such as viewing the situation from the client's perspective, the agency's perspective, or even a more global "community" perspective. Although the actual ratings may not change much between the different perspectives, it is possible that they will, and it is instructive to see where and to what extent they do.

In looking at the example Social Justice Scorecard shown in table 4.3, let us assume that we do not want to file any formal complaints with regulatory bodies or courts, preferring to first try to work with people in the community and the bank to improve the situation. We can hold the formal complaints and lawsuit option for later and use them as an implied "big stick" if our initial efforts for improvement do not work. Thus, the three alternative strategies listed are do nothing, change applicants' knowledge of banking procedures, and change bank hiring and training practices.

In this example, we have assigned a ranking that shows the degree to which each alternative addresses each of the four attributes of social justice. We are using a community-wide perspective in this example.

TABLE 4.3   Social Justice Scorecard for Policy Alternatives:
Bank Loan Example

Attributes of Social Justice	Alternative Strategies		
	Do Nothing	Change Applicants' Knowledge of Banking Procedures	Change Bank Hiring and Training Practices
Respect for Basic Human Rights	Low	Medium	Medium
Promotion of Social Responsibility	Low	Medium	High
Commitment to Individual Freedom	Low	Medium	Low
Support for Self-Determination	Low	Medium	Low

(Naturally, the ratings are subjective and others may rate them differently.) We believe that the "do nothing" strategy does not do much to improve any of the four attributes of social justice. We rate the "change applicants' knowledge of banking procedures" strategy as having a medium level of support for all four of the attributes. The final strategy, "change bank hiring and training practices," is medium in affecting respect for basic human rights, high in supporting promotion of social responsibility, and low in both commitment to individual freedom and support for self-determination.

From this initial review, it is clear that doing nothing will not promote social justice as much as either of the other strategies. There is not an obvious choice between the other two strategies, as their scores seem fairly close. To ease comparison, we can assign a number to each qualitative score, such as 1 for low, 2 for medium, and 3 for high. Then the "do nothing" strategy receives a score of 4, the "change applicants' knowledge" strategy receives a score of 8, and the "change bank hiring and training practices" strategy receives a score of 7. Thus, the second strategy has a slight edge in terms of our belief about how well it promotes social justice.

In this case, because the two strategies are not mutually exclusive, we might think of implementing both strategies for a more comprehensive attack on the problem. This also has the advantage of improving social justice overall, as each of the two alternatives has one or more areas that are better than the other alternative. Changing the hiring and training practices, for example, is better at promoting social responsibility for the issue, while changing applicants' knowledge of banking procedures is ranked higher for supporting self-determination.

Another option in using the Social Justice Scorecard is to assign weights to the different attributes. For example, if you believe that promotion of social responsibility is three times as important as each of the other attributes, then you would triple the score for that one attribute. In that case, the scores for each alternative strategy would be as follows: do nothing, $1 + 3 + 1 + 1 = 6$; change applicants' knowledge, $2 + 6 + 2 + 2 = 12$; and change bank hiring and training practices, $2 + 9 + 1 + 1 = 13$.

In this case, while the scores are still close for the two strategies of action, the strategy of changing bank hiring and training practices now has the slight edge. In order to keep the weighting process honest, it is important to select the relative weights *before* the ratings are decided upon.

CONCLUSION

This chapter has covered the important step of the advocacy practice process called understanding the issue. It is not possible to take action unless you understand the issue. This chapter has described a process of learning about and understanding the issue. The steps in the process are to define the issue, decide who is affected and how they are affected, decide what the main causes of the issue are, generate possible solutions to the issue, and review proposed solutions to determine their impact on social justice.

I have described several techniques to use to accomplish these steps, particularly ones for generating possible solutions to the issue and for evaluating the alternatives that have been generated. The steps and techniques described are equally useful whether the focus of advocacy is at the individual, group, community, or societal level.

Once the issue is understood, the next step in the advocacy practice approach is to actually plan the advocacy effort. This step is the subject of the next chapter.

Suggested Further Reading

Best, J. (2001). *Damned lies and statistics: Untangling numbers from the media, politicians and activists*. Berkeley, CA: University of California Press.

In this era of statistically driven policy debates, we all must learn how to critically examine what we are told by people with vested interests in having us believe them. This book is both a catalog of inaccurate "facts" that seem reasonable (but are not) and a primer on how to spot such errors on our own. Best provides a number of techniques to help us independently verify what we are told.

De Bono, E. (1999). *Six thinking hats*. Boston: Little, Brown.

This slim book presents an approach to improving decision making that is easy to understand and implement. Using this approach also can eliminate some of the arguing that occurs in meetings when different people approach a situation unknowingly wearing different hats. Although designed for groups, the approach also has application for individual problem solving and decision making.

Chapter 5

PLANNING IN
ADVOCACY PRACTICE

The students went to speak to their professor about their group paper grade. Their assignment had been to organize an advocacy project designed to help solve a social problem. The leader said, "This grade doesn't represent the amount of work and effort we put into this project. It just isn't fair." The professor, after teaching this course on advocacy all semester, was pleased that the students felt empowered enough to argue their grade, but he was sure that the grade was really fair, given the quality of the final product. "Okay," he said, "What do you want? What do you think a fair grade would be, and why?"

The students looked at one another in confusion. After some time, the leader finally mumbled, "Well, we want you to look it over again, I guess."

"That just proves you haven't learned much this semester," the professor declared. "You need to decide what you want from your advocacy effort and how to achieve it. Right now, you're just proving that the low grade is justified."

If you have ever been in a situation where you are asking someone with decision-making authority for something and you cannot explain what you want, you are a victim of a self-inflicted wound—a lack of planning. This chapter will provide information about what planning is, how to conduct it, and how to know when it is time to move to action. Premature action usually results in failure. Overly prolonged planning usually results in no change in the status quo. Both should be avoided.

The planning process is not something that you do on its own. It is predicated on the work that you have already done in getting involved, understanding the issue, developing possible solutions, and assessing those possible solutions. The planning process links together your previous work with a clearer focus on what outcomes you want to accomplish. After a full planning effort, you should be able to describe fully the answers to these four questions: What do you want? Who can get you what you want? When can, or should, you act? How can you act to get what you want?

Answering the first three questions provides the information needed to decide the answer to the last question. This chapter covers the first three questions, while chapters 6 and 7 answer the last question.

DEFINITION OF PLANNING

At its ultimately simplest level, planning is the process of deciding how to get from here to there. *Here* is the current situation, which we have already decided is inappropriate or unjust in some way and is certainly someplace we no longer want to be. *There*, on the other hand, is the future state of existence where the world will be improved, social justice will be more attained, and at least one person will be better off. We use a map to help us move from one physical location to another. It is also helpful to use a planning tool when we employ advocacy to get from here to there.

After much experience in getting from here to there in a particular physical location, we can often discard the map we have been using—we know how to get to work, how to get to the theater, how to get to places we usually go. Planning, however, is a tool we should use every time we engage in advocacy, because the "there" of each situation is never the same—even after we become very adept at the process of advocacy, each new advocacy effort is leading us to a different "there" and into an unknown future. Thus, we need to retain the mapping process when we engage in advocacy.

WHAT DO YOU WANT? USING ADVOCACY MAPPING TO DESCRIBE YOUR AGENDA

Without a clear understanding of what you want to accomplish, it is unlikely that you will achieve what you thought you wanted. As a problem-solving strategy, planning in advocacy must set forth goals to accomplish.

A tool derived from program planning and evaluation called a "logic model" is useful to the planning process (W. K. Kellogg Foundation, 2004). This model is an organized and succinct way to show the connections between what you plan to do and what you want to accomplish, including outcomes for the short-, medium- and long-term. An advocacy map will assist you in connecting what you want to achieve by engaging in advocacy with the tasks that you will engage in for that advocacy effort.

The advocacy map has several different sections (see fig. 5.1). Let us look at them one-by-one. The second line is labeled "Problem/ Issue." It is important to have a clear idea of what you are working to fix before you go any further. Considerable information was devoted to this topic in chapter 4, so it is now possible to fill in the problem/issue blank with what you have already decided.

The next line in an advocacy map is "Desired Outcome(s) for Client." This is what you would ideally like to see happen for the client. There are two important aspects about outcomes to which you must adhere. First, the outcome should indicate that the problem/issue has been resolved for the client. Second, but following from the first criteria, the outcome should be a change in the client's situation. This is your ideal, long-term outcome(s), not necessarily the one you believe is most likely or even likely at all, just the outcome(s) that would most improve the client's situation while being socially just. Be sure to write this as something positive and something that is a change in the client's situation.

Next we look at some examples of how to fill in these two lines. The following is an example of a poor problem statement: "My 14-year-old female client is not in the after-school class." The corresponding poor client outcome statement is as follows: "My client will be in the after-school class." At first glance, these may not seem too bad. The outcome statement is the opposite of the problem statement, and being in a class is a change in the client's situation—she was not in the class, and now she is. So, why are these poor statements for an advocacy map? The reason they are poor is that being in a class or not being in

FIGURE 5.1 The Advocacy Map

DATE: _____

Problem/Issue: _____

Desired Outcome(s) for Client: _____

Ultimate Social Justice–Related Outcome(s) for Society: _____

Resources (col. 1)	Tasks (col. 2)	Short-term Outcomes (col. 3)	Medium-term Outcomes (col. 4)	Long-term Outcomes (col. 5)	Ultimate Social Justice–Related Outcomes for Society (col. 6)

a class is usually *not* really the important aspect of a situation for a client—what *is* important is something that we can *know* is a negative thing. Being in a class may or may not be a negative thing. We do not really know why it is important for the student to be in the class, because we do not know what problem the client is facing. A better problem statement might be, "My client is engaging in risky behavior after school and before her mother gets home from work" (see fig. 5.2). This behavior is definitely a negative that we want to correct. Or, perhaps the issue is something else entirely and is better stated, "Discrimination based on race or sex is limiting choices for minority and female students at my client's school, including my client." This statement, too, indicates a situation that is negative. Either problem might be addressed by getting your client into the after-school class, but one can also think of other ways to address the problem as restated. If the problem statement remains, "My client is not in the after-school class," the range of solutions is limited to getting her into the class.

The next line in the advocacy map is "Ultimate Social Justice-Related Outcome(s) for Society." This line is where you connect the desired outcome for the client you are working with now to a society-wide change that would assist individuals or is the end result of all people having what you want for your current client. Using the above statements as examples, corresponding ultimate social justice-related outcomes for society might be: "All children will be in safe situations with nearby adult support." The other client outcome statement could lead to the following ultimate social justice-related outcome for society: "Discrimination based on race or sex will be eliminated."

The rest of the advocacy map is made up of six columns. Although the advocacy map reads from left to right, from the listing of resources to the listing of ultimate social justice-related outcomes, you can fill in the columns in any order that makes sense to you. We will fill it in, for the purpose of this example, from left to right, from "Resources" to "Ultimate Social Justice-Related Outcomes for Society."

It is often easy to list what resources are available (col. 1). This column is a listing of what is going to be used to solve the problem and address the issue. Resources include people (clients, their significant others, program staff, and volunteers), money, buildings, political support, other programs, and so on, that can be enlisted to achieve the

FIGURE 5.2 An Example Advocacy Map

DATE: _____

Problem/Issue: My client is engaging in risky behavior (unprotected sex and recreational use of marijuana) after school and before her mother gets home from work.

Desired Outcome(s) for Client: My client will not engage in risky behavior (unprotected sex and recreational use of marijuana) after school and before her mother gets home from work.

Ultimate Social Justice–Related Outcome(s) for Society: All children will be in safe situations with nearby adult support.

Resources (col. 1)	Tasks (col. 2)	Short-term Outcomes (col. 3)	Medium-term Outcomes (col. 4)	Long-term Outcomes (col. 5)	Ultimate Social Justice–Related Outcomes for Society (col. 6)
Student Client	• Search for acceptable alternative activities to the current risky behaviors • Research potential consequences of engaging in unprotected sex and recreational use of marijuana • Learn skills of advocacy for self and others	• Student will engage in other activities that do not put her at risk • Student will know negative potential consequences of unprotected sex, effects on later life chances of early pregnancy (for mother and child), and effects of marijuana on self and unborn child	• This student will have no more (or at least reduced) engagement in risky behaviors such as unprotected sex and drug use	• This student will not become pregnant and will discontinue use of all illegal drugs	• All children will be in safe situations with nearby adult support

Student Client's Parents	• Search for acceptable alternative activities to the current risky behaviors • Try to arrange situation so that greater supervision of client can be done by a parent or other trusted adult • If the after-school program is considered the best spot for their child, advocate for her to be placed in an appropriate situation (either at school or elsewhere)	• Student will engage in other activities that do not put her at risk • A parent or other trusted adult will be identified to supervise the student each day	• This student will have no more (or at least reduced) engagement in risky behaviors such as unprotected sex and drug use	• This student will not become pregnant and will discontinue use of all illegal drugs	• All children will be in safe situations with nearby adult support
Social Worker	• Search for acceptable alternative activities to the current risky behaviors • If the after-school program is considered the best spot for the client, advocate for client's inclusion in after-school activities program	• Student will engage in other activities that do not put her at risk • Program staff will allow student into program	• This student will have no more (or at least reduced) engagement in risky behaviors such as unprotected sex and drug use	• This student will not become pregnant and will discontinue use of all illegal drugs	• All children will be in safe situations with nearby adult support

Resources (col. 1)	Tasks (col. 2)	Short-term Outcomes (col. 3)	Medium-term Outcomes (col. 4)	Long-term Outcomes (col. 5)	Ultimate Social Justice-Related Outcomes for Society (col. 6)
Staff running the after-school activities program	• Allow this student into the program • Expand size of program to include all students who would benefit from the program	• Program staff will allow student into program • Program staff will have resources to work with all students who would benefit from the program	• This student will have no more (or at least reduced) engagement in risky behaviors such as unprotected sex and drug use	• This student will not become pregnant and will discontinue use of all illegal drugs • Female students in the program will not become pregnant and will not use illegal drugs	• All children will be in safe situations with nearby adult support

advocacy effort's desired outcomes. In the example advocacy map in figure 5.2, the resources listed are the client, the client's parents, the social worker handling the case, and the staff of the after-school activities program.

Each of these resources should have at least one task assigned (col. 2) to it. If there is no task to be done by a particular resource, there is no need for that particular resource in this advocacy effort. It should be noted that many of the resources may be assigned similar tasks, but as they come at the tasks from their different perspectives, the advocacy planner may need to coordinate efforts and mediate potential conflicts. If all goes well, the individual efforts will lead to more positive outcomes than what could be expected by any single resource's efforts.

An inanimate resource may have an important task, too. A resource such as a community center meeting room may have a task such as "provide a warm and inviting place for informal interaction among program staff and clients," although clearly a room by itself cannot do such a thing. This task would have to be combined with human resources.

In the example advocacy map in figure 5.2, almost every resource is assigned the task of searching for acceptable alternative activities for the client to engage in, including the client herself, the client's parents, and the social worker. Although it appears at this early planning stage that the best solution for the client is the after-school activities program at the school, this may not be true, so a thorough search for alternative solutions is to be conducted by the client, her parents, and the social worker. Some of the techniques in chapter 4 might be used to generate additional solutions. Only if this initial judgment that the after-school program would be beneficial is confirmed will additional efforts be made to enroll the girl in the program.

Each resource in this example also has at least one other task. The most common one is to learn to advocate or to actually advocate on behalf of the client.

Column 3, "Short-Term Outcomes," shows what the outcomes of the tasks should be. A short-term outcome is a change in a client's knowledge or behavior. There may not be a change in the client's objective, outward situation just yet, but the seeds are being planted for that to happen later. Short-term outcomes should happen shortly after the task is completed by the resource.

"Middle-term outcomes" (col. 4) are related to and follow directly from the short-term outcomes. They are often changes in behavior, though they may again be steps on the way to behavior change, such as changes in knowledge or attitude. The same middle-term outcome may have different short-term roots. In the example shown in figure 5.2, although there are many different short-term outcomes listed, all of them are thought to lead to the same middle-term outcome, reduction in or elimination of risky behavior by the client.

Column 5, "Long-Term Outcomes," continues the process of linking resources and their tasks to the accomplishment of getting to the desired "there" of the planning process. This column represents the stage where the problem/issue written at the beginning of the advocacy mapping process is fixed. This individual client, or this client group, now is living in a different situation than before. The map is showing the logical process of moving from the "here" to the "there" of successful advocacy.

Finally, we reach column 6, labeled "Ultimate Social Justice–Related Outcomes for Society." This column represents moving from the single case or group advocacy to global cause advocacy. This statement is linked to all the other desired outcomes and calls for considerable movement toward achieving social justice. It can be a rather large leap of faith from solving the problem of one or a few clients to changing the world, but it is important to consider the next steps beyond our initial client and where they can lead. In the case of figure 5.2, the ultimate social justice–related outcome for society is that all children will be in safe situations with nearby adult support. This statement is the same one that was created earlier and written above the set of columns in the advocacy map.

Another example of a completed advocacy map is shown in figure 5.3. In this case, the problem/issue is that of a client and her family experiencing hunger at the end of the month. In addition to this problem, they are considered ineligible for food from the emergency food bank due to an agency rule that says you can use the food bank only three times per year. The desired outcome for the client of this advocacy effort will be for the client and her family to have adequate

FIGURE 5.3 Example Advocacy Map

DATE: _____

Problem/Issue: My client and her family experience hunger regularly at the end of the month when cash runs low, and they have been ruled ineligible for continued assistance because they have received groceries from the emergency food bank three times already this year.

Desired Outcome(s) for Client: My client and her family will have adequate amounts of nutritious food throughout the month.

Ultimate Social Justice–Related Outcome(s) for Society: A society where everyone has adequate amounts of nutritious food.

Resources (col. 1)	Tasks (col. 2)	Short-term Outcomes (col. 3)	Medium-term Outcomes (col. 4)	Long-term Outcomes (col. 5)	Ultimate Social Justice–Related Outcomes for Society (col. 6)
Client and family members	• Research about other sources of resources • Fill in other program applications	• Informed about other resources • Completed applications	• Clients are deemed eligible for food assistance	• Receive adequate amounts of nutritious food • Self-supporting, in terms of food	• A society where everyone has adequate amounts of nutritious food
Social worker	• Provide knowledge of programs to clients • Assist client in program applications	• Client learns about possible programs • Social worker is aware of policies of program and the constraints of the agency	• Clients make choices about how to overcome lack of food	• Client has improved knowledge of system and how to access it appropriately	• A society where everyone has adequate amounts of nutritious food

Resources (col. 1)	Tasks (col. 2)	Short-term Outcomes (col. 3)	Medium-term Outcomes (col. 4)	Long-term Outcomes (col. 5)	Ultimate Social Justice–Related Outcomes for Society (col. 6)
	• Advocate to emergency relief program to see if family can receive additional food • Push for more adequate funding for food programs	• Social worker knows of need for more funding of program	• Social worker tries to influence policies in other organizations and advocates for larger program budgets	• Advocacy targets learn more about program needs • Agencies receive additional resources for food aid programs	
Community programs, such as food banks	• Agencies disclose all rules and procedures for collecting and distributing food	• Programs agree to review rules and procedures to determine if they could be improved	• Within agency constraints, benefits are increased—in any case, benefits are distributed as equitably as possible	• Agencies self-monitor their policies and procedures, putting social justice at the fore	• A society where everyone has adequate amounts of nutritious food
Government programs, such as food stamps	• Advocate pushes legislators and agency to examine laws, rules, and procedures for providing benefits	• Legislators/program staff agree to review rules and procedures	• Within agency constraints, benefits are increased—in any case, they are distributed as equitably as possible	• Agencies self-monitor their policies and procedures, putting social justice at the fore	• A society where everyone has adequate amounts of nutritious food

amounts of nutritious food throughout the month. Ultimately, the social justice-related outcome for society is that everyone has adequate amounts of nutritious food.

Columns 1 through 6 are filled in, using the guidelines described earlier. Still, it seems clear that the entries are somewhat more "macro" focused compared to the example in figure 5.2. This difference is not a problem. The advocacy mapping process is flexible and has few hard and fast rules. The key aspect of the technique to focus on is to lay out a series of implicit if-then statements. For example, *if* the client searches for information on additional programs, *then* her knowledge of possible options will be greater. *If* the social worker provides information on the dangers of unprotected sex, *then* the client will not engage in unprotected sex.

Naturally, not all of these if-then statements seem as strong or as likely as others, but the use of an advocacy map will make clear the strong and weak points of the planning logic. By laying out the desired resources, tasks, and expected outcomes, everyone involved in the planning process can better determine how strong the connections are and if they need to be strengthened further before proceeding.

Tips on Developing Advocacy Maps

Some wonder who should develop the advocacy map. It works best when as many of the people you are counting on as resources can be involved as possible. After all, most of us work more diligently and with more enthusiasm on a plan that we have been a part of developing. This level of involvement also fits in well with the social work value of client self-determination.

Another issue to consider is the amount of detail to include, particularly in the outcomes columns. This will vary from one set of planners and from one set of circumstances to another. Outcomes, by their nature, however, are signposts or milestones on the way to a more distant goal. Although some specificity is needed to know if you have reached a desired point on the way from "here" to "there," those planning an advocacy effort must also leave room for unexpected detours and delays. Thus, advocacy maps are usually best seen as maps of major features along the way rather than detailed maps of every road and street. They are both strategic and tactical in nature, becoming more strategic the farther to the right on the page we go.

Another practical tip is to date each version of the advocacy map. Things will change as you move along, no matter how easy the project seems at its inception. Resources will appear and disappear, people will reevaluate what their contribution is going to be, and new conditions will emerge. To make sure you are working from the most current advocacy map, experience shows that a date on the page is very important.

The advocacy mapping process forces the planners to determine what their desired outcomes are. Determination of desired outcomes is similar to setting your agenda (Richan, 1996). What it does not do a good job of, however, is to set forth which of these outcomes is more important than others, what Richan calls "setting priorities." Those involved in the advocacy effort should engage in a discussion of the relative importance of the various outcomes. Everyone should agree on which of the desired outcomes can be jettisoned in order to accomplish other more valuable outcomes.

Prioritizing Outcomes

Your advocacy map contains a number of outcomes—short-term, medium-term, and long-term for each of the resources you have identified. Although there is clearly overlap between these outcomes, they are not all the same. Thus, you must prioritize them. Some are more important than others. Some are less important, or merely instrumental, that is, important only because they lead to something else considered important. It is helpful to prioritize the outcomes within each column rather than between columns. In other words, rank all the outcomes at the short-term level against each other, for example, rather than comparing a short-term outcome to a long-term outcome.

This step can be quite difficult, as the outcomes are all important, or else they probably would not have been included in the advocacy map to begin with. The purpose of the prioritization is to make the advocate aware of where the most time and attention should be placed. Given limited resources for any advocacy effort, it makes sense to begin with trying to achieve the most important outcomes. In addition, an important part of the advocacy process is knowing that most advocates do not achieve everything that they would like to in any one effort. It may take several efforts to achieve even one or two of the desired outcomes. Thus, if it comes to having to trade off one potential outcome in order to achieve another one, it is vital to know which outcomes are more important.

After this process of figuring out what you want, you are now ready to answer the second question of the planning process: Who can get you what you want?

WHO CAN GET WHAT YOU WANT?
IDENTIFYING YOUR TARGET

Another element of the planning process that up to now has been more implicit than explicit is the identification of the target, that is, the person who can make the decision that the advocacy effort seeks. The target is the ultimate recipient of the advocacy effort, even if others are contacted as intermediaries in the advocacy process. As the advocacy map is developed, it often becomes clear who your target should be. If it is not clear, the planners will need to make this more explicit. It may take some time and effort to determine who, indeed, can make the desired decision. If you change your mind as to who this person is, be prepared to change the advocacy map as you go along. Like all planning documents, it presents the best plan at the time it is created. The map should not be considered unchangeable.

The choice of the target may not be as easy as it first seems. The following is a well-explained description of the situation:

> ... in a complex, interrelated, urban society, it becomes increasingly difficult to single out who is to blame for any particular evil. There is a constant, and somewhat legitimate, passing of the buck.... One big problem is a constant shifting of responsibility from one jurisdiction to another—individuals and bureaus one after another disclaim responsibility for particular conditions, attributing the authority for any change to some other force. (Alinsky, 1972, p. 130–131)

This shifting of blame can happen within an agency when an advocate tries to alter policy, and it certainly happens when larger scale problems occur. Your supervisor cannot make the decision you want her to because it contradicts agency policy. The agency director points the finger at her board of directors for making poor policy choices but says her hands are tied. The board indicates that it is acting on legal advice related to local government edicts. Local officials blame state government for policy decisions they enforce; everyone complains about the federal government, claiming that the laws and rules that are handed down are "out of touch" with reality. Who, then, should be the target?

This is the time to return to your advocacy map to determine who, indeed, can get you what you want. Start with short-term objectives. Who can make the decision or start action on the outcomes that are the most immediately desired? Once these are accomplished, it may be possible to find the right target(s) for the medium-term and long-term outcomes.

At times, though, you may feel you are in the policy equivalent of a telephone answering system where you keep pushing buttons for other options and never are able to reach a human being who can take your call. In this case, Alinksy (1972) advises "freezing" the target—picking one person and making him or her the personification of the issue. Given enough pressure, the person may be able to find a creative way to take effective action in order to get away from being the target. One must be careful, however, when trying to freeze the target within your own job setting, as it may cause problems for you in your work.

For many advocacy situations, however, finding one person to personify the issue may not be feasible because it will take a group of people (such as a city council or other legislative body) to make a collective decision if you are to get what you want. In this case, the legislature is your target. Still, you will need to convince only a majority of the legislature to adopt your viewpoint, not the entire organization. Because the legislature is made up of individuals, you must figure out how to reach these men and women, your targets, within the larger body.

Now that you know what you want and you think you know who can get you what you want, you must decide when to act.

WHEN, CAN, OR SHOULD YOU ACT?

Napoleon Bonaparte, former emperor of France, once said, "Take time to deliberate, but when the time for action has arrived, stop thinking and go in." In most cases, no "witching hour" or "magic time" is going to happen. There is no perfect moment, that moment when victory is assured, for advocacy. When the planning is done to an adequate level to make it clear what resources are available, what tasks are to be done, what outcomes are to be achieved, and who can get you what you want, no reason for delay exists. The time to act is now.

Sometimes you cannot do what needs to be done immediately. You may have to schedule a meeting to talk with the target, or you many need to wait for a public hearing that is already scheduled before you can speak out. But there are, nonetheless, actions you can take today to prepare for what will come later.

Delaying taking action to achieve the outcomes you have developed is often due to anxiety or fear. It is natural to want to avoid taking steps that require you to move beyond your usual routine, even if you are a seasoned advocate. Focusing on the desired outcomes, however, moves your focus from you and your feelings to the better world waiting for your client and the increased realization of social justice that you can make happen. Reminding yourself of the larger goals of your planned advocacy effort often is enough to rekindle a desire to act and to act now.

CONCLUSION

This chapter has described the importance of planning in advocacy. I introduced advocacy maps as a tool for thinking about and communicating an advocacy effort. In an advocacy map, resources and tasks are linked to desired outcomes that will achieve a better situation for the immediate client and also for society at large, as social justice goals are considered and worked toward.

Once the planning stage is completed, it is time to act. The next chapter provides information on how to get what you want.

Suggested Further Reading

W. K. Kellogg Foundation (2004). *Logic model development guide*. Battle Creek, MI: W. K. Kellogg Foundation.

This publication presents an in-depth look at what logic modes are, how they are used throughout the life of a program (from design to evaluation and renewal), and how to develop them. The advocacy map described in this chapter is an adaptation of the versatile and useful logic model.

Chapter 6

ADVOCATING THROUGH
NEGOTIATION AND PERSUASION

Never get angry. Never make a threat. Reason with people. Don
Corleone, *The Godfather*

Advocating involves many skills, each coming together in pursuit
of the desired outcomes designated on the advocacy map. So far in this
book, I have covered skills such as analysis, planning, and idea generation. Still, no advocacy has yet occurred because no one has been
approached with an idea that you want them to adopt. What will happen when you actually have a decision maker listening to you or reading your material? How can you make the most of the limited time you
have to make an impact?

Two of the most important skills at this stage of advocacy are negotiation and persuasion. Both rely on having appropriate information.
This chapter covers negotiation and persuasion and also describes how
an advocate must gather useful information and employ different
approaches to persuasion and negotiation, depending on the target of
the advocacy. Without knowing how to negotiate and how to be persuasive, an advocate will find it difficult to make a difference.

NEGOTIATION

"*Negotiation* is any communication in which you are attempting
to achieve the approval, acquiescence, or action of someone else"
(Donaldson & Donaldson, 1996, p. 1). Thus, advocacy is, by its nature,
also negotiation. Negotiation frequently takes place as a conversation of
sorts, in which positions are stated in order to find one that everyone
can accept. Simple advocacy negotiations can involve two busy people
discussing when to set up a meeting; more complex negotiations

involve many coalition partners deciding what should be included in a piece of legislation. This section describes some of the key elements of negotiation.

One of the first rules in any negotiation is that you are unlikely to get everything that you want. That is one reason that prioritization (discussed in chap. 5) is so important. Knowing what is more important and what is less important in your advocacy effort means that it is easier to choose which outcomes to give up in order to achieve the more important ones. When prioritizing outcomes, negotiators develop their "limit," their "initial position," and their "fallback positions."

Limit

A limit is the worst possible offer by the other side that is still acceptable. When the other side in a negotiation offers less than your limit and sticks to that as the final offer, you know that it is better to walk away than to accept the offer. The benefit of deciding your limit before starting negotiations is that you will not have to make such a weighty decision while bargaining. Deciding what you cannot accept while you have time to consider issues in an unpressured environment will lead to better decision making later on. Naturally, you hope to achieve a better result than just your limit.

Initial Positions

Initial positions are the first thing you say when you are asked what you want. Initial positions ask for more than what you expect to get, but they are presented to provide a starting point and some room to negotiate. An initial position should be reasonably ambitious, but not so outlandish that the person on the other side of the deliberations feels it is totally ridiculous. An outlandish initial position could get the negotiation process off to a very bad start. In general, negotiators prefer to get the other side to reveal its opening position first. If the other side opens with an offer that is better than you thought you could achieve, you have the upper hand and can probably walk away from the negotiation session very pleased. Even if that ideal situation does not occur, some people believe that whoever talks first loses by revealing his opening position. Naturally, however, someone has to go first.

The best negotiators ask a lot of questions to gain information from the other person (Bedell, 2000). The most obvious way to invite the other person to begin is to ask what she hopes to attain in the negotiation. Sometimes this is too broad a question, so you can provide additional information about what type of answer you are looking for. This process, called "signaling" (Bedell), requires that you narrow the question.

Imagine you are working with a coalition partner, putting together an agenda for the upcoming legislative session. Instead of asking, for example, "What would you like to attain in this negotiation?" you could ask, "Given that we are trying to determine the legislative priorities for the coalition, what are three points that are very important to you?" (It is better to say "very important" rather than "most important" because it keeps the other person from being locked into particular points being *most* important. If points are *most* important, then they have to be included in the bill or your counterpart may feel he has lost something in the negotiations and then seek to undermine the outcome.) This question cues an appropriate answer and allows for a meaningful beginning to negotiations. You could find already existing areas of agreement between your positions and use them to work for further agreement.

Another tactic is "bat listening," or echolocation (Bedell, 2000). With this tactic, if you do not receive enough information from your negotiating partner, you send out a signal and listen closely to what comes back in order to determine your next move. Suppose you are working with your son's teacher to improve your son's school performance. You know you want him not to be labeled as "learning disabled," and you want him to either be held back a year or have extra assistance from the school counselor. You do not know what the teacher is going to recommend. But you suspect that she does not want to spend extra time on your child, given her other duties and the large number of children in her class who might also want extra attention. If the teacher seems adamant about putting the onus on you to start the ball rolling, you might say, "Putting extra effort into helping a student takes time away from your other duties, doesn't it?" This leading statement allows her to vent her anxieties about what you might want from her. You can then discuss your ideas with a better sense of her concerns. If she does not respond much, you can try again, looking for an issue that will start her talking. This type of interaction is one most social workers are good at and have been trained to do.

An advantage of this process is that it also allows people to talk about their personal needs (which are always important, whether mentioned or not) rather than their "official needs." In this case, the official need is for your son to do better in school. Although that need is undoubtedly important to the teacher, she may feel even more strongly that she does not want a personal need violated, namely, the need to accomplish all her other duties in a timely way, which is how the principal is going to judge her performance.

A third approach is called "looking forward." This approach brings out what the end result of the negotiation should be. For example, you might say, "Let's project into the future. What do you visualize as the ideal outcome? How would things work? How would things work if you could write the script and everything went as you'd like it to go?" (Bedell, 2000, p. 66).

A fourth technique reverses "looking forward" to "looking back." In this approach, the questions that are asked bring out what the other person does not like about the current or past situation. An example of using this technique is if you were working with members of a community group who are reluctant to attend a meeting at city hall to present testimony to the city council. Members of the group went once and did not care for the experience. Before you can convince them to do something that you find absolutely essential to the advocacy effort, you need to know what they did not like and what changes they would like to see.

The final way to address the dilemma of getting the other side to go first is to ignore the rule, at least partially. This approach is called the "What do you think of this?" technique (Bedell, 2000). You begin by stating one of the parts of your opening position (assuming you have more than one part) and letting the other person react to it. You can actually use the question "What do you think of that?" The other person usually will counter with an initial position that is less than you want. And so the negotiation game starts in earnest. Of course, you should try to persuade your target of the validity of your position. After all, you have not adopted an initial position that is wholly unreasonable. Your initial position should have a basis in reality, even if it represents a better-than-expected result for the negotiation. Do not be too quick to abandon it.

Once that point has been discussed, even if no firm agreement has been reached, you can ask the other person to lay out her side's other desires. If she is reluctant, you can point out that you got the ball rolling on the previous point, and so it is only fair for her to take the lead on this topic. You can also use the "What do you think of that?" technique again, if all else fails.

One of the important elements of negotiation is that we often have to negotiate with our friends. Advocacy is not just about facing opponents—oftentimes advocates must negotiate agreements with people who are basically on their side but perhaps do not see things in exactly the same way.

Fallback Positions

Fallback positions are also standard in any negotiation. They are concessions that you make in order to keep the negotiation moving. Fallback positions get you less than the initial position but still represent an acceptable result for the advocacy effort. Your target, if well prepared, also has a set of concessions. Sometimes in the negotiation process you link keeping something you want with letting the target get something. Some of your fallback positions should be the outcomes in your advocacy map. You should also have one or more fallback positions that are less desired than the outcomes on your advocacy map if such results would, nonetheless, represent acceptable progress.

Only you can determine how quickly to move from your initial position to one of your fallback positions. If you cave immediately, you run the risk of seeming to be either a weak negotiator or unprepared. If you hold out too long, however, you run the risk of blocking progress as the target hardens his or her stance as well. The best results can often be achieved by making a minor concession on one of your lower priority points and then taking cues from your target's behavior about how quickly to make or to demand future concessions.

At some point, you may run out of concessions you are willing to make. This means you have reached your limit—the point at which not continuing to negotiate, and achieving no agreement at all, is preferable to agreeing to the target's offer. Your limit can be determined by only you and others involved in the advocacy effort. If the proposal on the table worsens matters for your client, if it means that your long-term efforts toward social justice are harmed, or if it does not achieve anything worthwhile for the investment of time and energy you have made, it may be time to walk away. Sometimes just the act of preparing to walk away loosens the target up to more concessions. But you cannot count on that. So, if you indicate that you have reached your limit, you *must* be willing to end negotiations if no concessions are forthcoming.

This information on negotiation provides the framework for what you want to accomplish, but it does not provide you with information on how to conduct the negotiation or how to get your target to agree to your positions. That topic, the art of persuasion, is covered in the next section.

PERSUASION

Persuasion is a more powerful method of advocacy than negotiation. In negotiation you and the other party make a series of concessions, which implies that neither side gets what it really wants. In persuasion, however, you are able to get the other party to do what you want. (There are other ways of getting others to do what you want, such as coercion, but this book does not cover those other ways.) In persuasion, one party gets all of what it wants, and the other side, by agreeing to a new position, also gets what it wants.

Recent research on persuasion treats it as a goal-oriented behavior (Wilson, 2002). A considerable amount is known about what is important when attempting to influence. In every attempt at persuasion, four important variables are the context, the message, the sender, and the receiver. I discuss these variables next.

The Context

The context of the advocacy attempt determines most of the content used. How the situation is viewed by each actor establishes, to a large extent, his or her reaction to it. Various terms have been used to describe the process of getting a particular viewpoint accepted as the "right" way to see a situation—one often used in the political world is *spin*. *Spin* is a negative term often used in the political world to describe putting the best face on facts in order to reach a predetermined outcome. Another, less loaded, term for the same process is *framing* (Rhoads, 1997). "A frame is a psychological device that offers a perspective and manipulates salience in order to influence subsequent judgment" (Rhoads). A frame thus provides a certain standpoint on how the facts should be seen, emphasizing some facts and minimizing others in order to get the recipient to act a certain way. A frame highlights some information as being important to consider, while filtering out other information that does not fit in. Framing occurs in policy arguments. For example, is domestic violence a personal problem or a community problem? Is poverty caused by flawed character or by restricted opportunities? (Schiller, 2004). Shifting images of issues actually lead to rapid changes in laws and regulations (Baumgartner & Jones, 1993). So, the ability to frame a debate advantageously is often enough to win the debate.

Framing a decision makes people more likely to act in a certain manner. People are much less willing to suffer a loss than they are to go for an equal gain (Kahneman & Tversky, 1990). There is evidence that the way choices are laid out, even if functionally the same, affects decisions (Kahneman & Tversky). Eating a hamburger that is 75 percent lean, for example, sounds more appealing than eating one that is 25 percent fat. Eating escargot is more alluring than eating snails. Shakespeare, it seems, was wrong—a rose by any other name probably would *not* smell as sweet.

There are several typical frames that advocates use to define an issue or proposal that are actually borrowed from Rosenthal's (1993) "public policy rhetoric." Five of these frames are useful to kill an idea, and one is useful to promote an idea. I also list and explain three others that are likely to promote a good image for a proposal.

"It isn't fair." In the first frame, proposals are tagged "unfair" to one group or another. Almost any proposal an advocate comes up with—from helping one client more than others to economic policy that affects global trading—can be called unfair. A newspaper article describing views of tax policy shows how frequently this frame is put forward (Benson, 2004). Grover Norquist, president of Americans for Tax Reform, is quoted, "Flat taxes treat everybody the same. If the gov-

ernment is going to want some of your dollars, it should take the same from everybody. It's a question of equity" (Benson, p. E4). In the same article, David Cay Johnston, author of *Perfectly Legal*, states, "We have a system in which some already wealthy people don't want to contribute to maintaining the society that has made their wealth possible. They want you to take on the burden for them, and they hire people to argue that what they want is good for you" (Benson, p. E4).

"It won't work." An alternative frame used to argue against a proposal is that whatever goal it is trying to achieve will not be reached. An idea you have, for example, to improve intake procedures at your organization could be met with responses such as, "We've tried that before. The problem is that clients are just too lazy to get all their paperwork together before coming in for their intake interview." Not only has your proposal been attacked, but an alternative frame has been provided that blames clients for the problem. This frame is sometimes also presented with the following argument: "That sounds good in theory, but it just doesn't work like that in the real world."

"It can be done in other ways." In arguing against a proposal, you may also say, "it can be done in other ways." This frame is similar to the previous one, although it presents an alternative to what it cuts down. This approach to attacking a proposal has a long history and is enshrined in *Robert's Rules of Order* (Robert, Evans, Honeman, & Balch, 2000) as a "substitute motion," whereby one idea is totally eliminated in favor of another. The Patient's Bill of Rights is an example of this approach. Democrats had much popular support for improving the rights of patients vis-à-vis health maintenance organizations (HMOs) that covered their health care costs. Seeing that the Democrats were likely to make an election-year issue out of the Republicans' lack of support for such an idea, the Republicans put together a different package of legislative ideas, calling it *their* Patient's Bill of Rights. It was claimed that this new bill was better than the Democrats' proposal and was subsequently voted into law by the Republican Congress. Republicans thus finally said that although the Democrats had a point, their goals could be better accomplished in a different way.

"It costs too much." Another frame is to say, "it costs too much." If an advocate's idea is stuck with this rhetorical tag, the proposal is going to have a difficult and probably short life. Particularly in times of government cuts to existing programs, new ideas are tough to fund. But belt-tightening occurs in every organization, no matter its size, and there is always pressure to keep costs low. New ideas that have significant financial repercussions may not ever be seriously considered, much less adopted. Agency managers will say, "I think that sounds like a good idea, if only the budget could support it." Elected officials argue that "the days of big government are over" and want to reduce taxes. Sometimes advocates are challenged to come up with a way to pay for their idea. Even when viable funding approaches are provided, however, the advocate frequently hears one of the other negative frames aimed at her idea.

"It will hurt the public and/or clients." Sometimes this frame is a variation of "it costs too much" or "it isn't fair." Often, however, it has a life of its own. When the Texas social work licensure board was threatened with elimination or consolidation with other professional licensure boards, the state chapter of the National Association of Social Workers argued that due to the unique nature of the social work profession the lack of a licensure board just for social workers would potentially harm the public. When a neighborhood organization wanted to prevent rezoning that would put a convenience store and gas station in a residential and park-filled area, the advocates argued that changes to the environment, increases in crime and alcohol use, and decreased property value would hurt the public. This frame can be extended to intra-agency debates by arguing that a new idea or administrative rule will harm the organization's clients.

The above five frames are typical when trying to shoot down an idea. The following four frames (the first from Rosenthal, 1993, p. 194, the rest original) are used to support a proposal.

"It will help consumers and/or clients." Deregulation of the trucking and airline industries was promoted as a way to increase choice and lower prices. Many proposals are set forth with the idea that consumers will be offered more for less. At the agency level, many

advocates focus on the benefits their suggestions will have for clients. After all, in the NASW Code of Ethics (1999), the first value listed is "service," and the first ethical principle is, "Social workers' primary goal is to help people in need and to address social problems." If a plan is seen as beneficial to clients, it is difficult to derail it in a social service organization.

"The benefits outweigh the costs." The cost of an idea is often cited as a reason not to adopt it. The seasoned advocate learns to expect such an attack and frequently counterattacks with this frame. In this context, advocates talk about the difference between short-term and long-term thinking and accounting. When legislators wanted to reduce the state budget in Texas, one program they targeted was the Children's Health Insurance Program. Advocates who wanted to maintain the program's funding argued two main points. First, because the federal government provided three dollars for every state dollar, cutting state expenditures on this program was a terrible way to save money. Second, the costs of not attending to children's health care needs when they are young show up later in life and are then much more expensive to treat. Another example of the use of this frame is the following slogan: "If you think education is expensive, you should see how much ignorance costs."

"If it saves the life of one child, it will all be worth it." This frame unashamedly pulls at heartstrings. It says that costs might be high, but it challenges anyone to say that life, particularly an innocent child's life, is less precious than gold. Will it be expensive to install a school crossing sign, put up chain-link fencing around the perimeter, and provide a school crossing guard every day? Perhaps. But what is more important than the safety of our children?

"After what they've gone through, they deserve it." The argument here acknowledges that the outcomes of the idea might not be fair in some sense because some people will get more than others. Yet there is an element of fairness involved, because the people who are getting more (money, services, opportunities) have also earned it by what they have gone through. This frame is a strong argument for some

groups of people, like those who have served in the armed forces and have clearly put themselves at risk for the benefit of all. Other groups who might be labeled, generically, as victims may also be able to use this advocacy approach, particularly if they are seen as not contributing to their own situation. Widows, orphans, crime victims, people who have nature to blame for a calamity, and others who have had ill luck may find this approach to be a powerful frame. This conflict is sometimes called the equality of outcome (everyone ends up similarly in the end) versus equity (people get what they deserve) debate and is based on different approaches to what is considered fair.

The importance of framing in advocacy cannot be overstated. In order for you to have a chance at being persuasive, the target must accept your framing of the issue. If your frame differs from the target's, a great deal of effort should be spent in getting him or her to alter his or her view of the issue. Similarly, you must be careful not to uncritically accept someone else's view of a situation. Implicit assumptions regarding your clients' deservedness or different views on social justice may be influencing your target to see the situation you are advocating about in a very different way than you do. Make sure to understand what frame your target is using when listening to what he or she states and proposes.

The Message

The message the advocate sends to the target is the information that is designed to be persuasive. Here, we look at characteristics of the message rather than the content of the message. Nonverbal signals, as well as verbal, are part of the message, but those will be covered in the next section, which describes the sender. The content of the message is also clearly important, but that is covered in chapter 7.

Six general principles of persuasive messages are discussed in this section: intent, organization, sidedness, repetition and redundancy, rhetorical questions, and fear appeals. This discussion is based largely on Booth-Butterfield (1996), although the examples are original.

Intent. In most cases it is counterproductive to announce your intent, that you are going to try to influence someone. The moment the target hears your intent, defensive walls start going up, and justifications for past behavior are mentally rehearsed. It is better to begin the persuasion effort without forewarning the person whose mind you want to change. There are two important exceptions to this general guideline, however. The first is when you want to ask for only small changes, knowing that the message receivers already agree with most of what you are about to say. Thus, by saying that you want to ask only for incremental change, resistance is lowered. The target feels safer, knowing that you do not want to shake things up too much.

The second exception is when your target already expects you to attempt persuasion. Thus, in most structured office visits or telephone conversations with elected officials, it does not hurt to say you are going to try to influence their opinion, because they know that is why you have come in or called. Admitting the purpose of the conversation recognizes the intelligence of the target and lets the advocate seem more honest.

Organization. Well-organized messages are more persuasive than are poorly organized messages. This point seems too obvious to mention, yet there is always a temptation for advocates to hurry up and get going, neglecting the preparation and organizing phase of the message. It is worth taking the time to make key points more salient and to ensure a logical consistency in the material. If the message is not perfectly organized, however, all is not lost. Minor discrepancies generally do not cause targets to have much trouble comprehending or being persuaded by messages.

Sidedness. The next principle to consider is sidedness. When should advocates present both sides of an issue, and when should they present only their side? The research shows that two-sided messages (those that present the position advocated and the opposing view) are more persuasive if they do two things: they must defend the desired position *and* attack the other position. If the other position is mentioned but not attacked, there is no advantage to the two-sided presentation as compared to a one-sided presentation (Cialdini, 2000).

The reason for these results is that a two-sided message appears more fair and balanced. Because most people do not think deeply about most issues, presenting the other side makes the advocate seem more credible. Even if the target is thinking deeply about the issue being presented, the combination of defense and attack gets that person thinking even more about the issue. The attack on the other side and the defense of the advocate's position can leave a lasting impression of having explored the issue completely. If the reasons provided are strongly in favor of your position, you may be successful in your persuasion effort.

Repetition and redundancy. Repetition and redundancy are different, though closely related. *Repetition* refers to communicating the same thing over and over. *Redundancy*, on the other hand, refers to having multiple ways of communicating similar information. A redundant message repeats the major theme of other messages but does it in a different way. Think of a redundant message as a back-up plan. If the first message did not get the target's attention, maybe the next one will.

A little repetition adds a lot of persuasion power, because it can take several communication attempts for information to sink in. You cannot assume that all the information you are trying to push will be heard the first time. After some time, however, simple repetition of a message creates frustration on the part of the target, causing him to think, "Oh, no—I'm going to hear all about her pet project again!" You, as the advocate, must sense when this frustration effect begins to interfere with your being heard. At that point, you should switch to a redundant message, which presents the original (or slightly altered) message in a new package.

Rhetorical questions. The use of rhetorical questions is very effective, isn't it? Advocates who understand the science of persuasion achieve more results, don't they? Rhetorical questions are disguised statements—they stake out a position without appearing to and can be backed away from if opposition emerges. Research shows that the use of rhetorical questions can change how people think (Cialdini, 2000). Rhetorical questions can catch people off guard if they are not paying full attention and pull them back to awareness of what you are saying. If you use rhetorical questions late in a presentation, targets often understand them as a "persuasion cue," indicating a correct position. This effect is particularly strong if the topic is not of great interest or importance to them. In these conditions, targets assume that evidence has already been presented that show these "statements" to be true and that they just missed the evidence.

Fear appeals. A fear appeal is a message that focuses on the bad things that will happen if you do or do not do something. The message indicates that you better do whatever it is that the advocate is suggesting in order to avoid some sort of catastrophe. You are probably familiar with advertising that uses this technique:

> Buy our life insurance or your loved ones will live in desperate poverty when you die!
> Don't drink and drive or you may end up in a fiery, burning car wreck, killing yourself or someone else!
> Use our shampoo or people will shun you for having dandruff!

The same kind of appeal can be used in advocacy:

> If you do not pass this bill, millions of children will be without health insurance, leading to huge financial burdens placed on local charitable hospitals!
> If the board makes that decision, we may be liable in court for large sums of money!
> If a gasoline station is built near a river supplying water to the town, a gas spill could pollute millions of gallons of water, making it unsafe for human consumption!

It is thought that the reason fear appeals are effective is that they motivate greater thinking about the topic. When a situation is described in a way that increases fear, a natural reaction is to want to take action to protect oneself against that threat. In order to work, however, not only must a person feel a realistic and personal fear of negative consequences, but the appeal must also provide information about a feasible action the target can take to avoid those consequences. In other words, you cannot just scare people into action; you must also guide them in the way to safety.

This section has covered ways to shape the advocate's message so that it is more persuasive. There are also principles that apply to the advocate herself, the message's sender. I cover them next.

The Sender

No matter how you shape your message, using the ideas from the previous section, a considerable amount of your ability to be persuasive is dependent on aspects of you, the advocate, and how you are perceived by your audience. This section emphasizes the role of credibility. To be persuasive, you must be believable. Without credibility, an advocate is not going to persuade anyone. Credibility, however, is a multidimensional concept comprised of three factors: expertise, trustworthiness, and likeability.

Having expertise about the issue for which you are advocating is important to be persuasive, but it is not enough by itself. In fact, if the target already has a strong position on an issue or is distracted from the expert's presentation, all the expertise in the world will do little good. The testimony of an expert is most effective when the target does not care too much about the issue or does not have the capacity to counter argue, such as from a lack of sleep or because the topic is complex and the listener is overwhelmed. In either condition, the target uses the expert's ideas as a shortcut to thinking for himself (Perloff, 1993).

Several ways to improve your perceived expertise exist. One is to have a title associated with expertise: professors and doctors immediately have more expertise than ordinary people do. If the person has won a prestigious award, such as the Nobel Prize, a halo effect is created. For example, Linus Pauling, 1954 Nobel Prize winner in chemistry for his work on the genetic influences on sickle cell anemia and 1962 Nobel Peace Prize winner, is perhaps most well remembered today for his efforts to promote the use of megadoses of vitamin C. Pauling's advocacy of vitamin C has been accepted based on his endorsement. People assumed that, because he had two Nobel prizes, he must know what he was talking about. Pauling preached that large amounts of vitamin C helped to prevent colds and other illnesses (including cancer), despite a lack of scientific evidence to support this idea. The outcome of Pauling's halo effect has been dramatic: "Thanks largely to Pauling's prestige, annual vitamin C sales in the United States have been in the hundreds of millions of dollars for many years. The physical damage to people he led astray cannot be measured" (Barrett, 2001). Many professionals hang their diplomas, licenses, or other credentials in their offices to promote their expertise. People without such credentials may offer other proofs of expertise, such as testimonial letters.

Another way to demonstrate expertise is to talk like an expert. Using the language of a field is an important element of being an expert. You have to be able to talk the talk, which means knowing the jargon. One study even showed that an expert was seen as more credible when speaking in complex, difficult-to-understand terms than when the same content was conveyed using more ordinary language (Cooper, Bennett, & Sukel, 1996). This research indicates that "Acknowledged experts may be most persuasive when nonexperts can't understand the details of what they are saying" (Rhoads & Cialdini, 2002, p. 516). Although this is an empirically validated way to be persuasive, it runs counter to social work ethics. Still, it is important to know that this technique works in order to guard against it.

The difference between expertise and trustworthiness is important, but both are vital to being an effective advocate. Whereas expertise indicates that you know what you are talking about, trustworthiness indicates that you are honest and lack bias (Rhoads & Cialdini, 2002). Because of the central role of trustworthiness in establishing credibility, it is a key duty of advocates to develop an image of trustworthiness in the eyes of their targets.

Trust can be developed over time as the result of many interactions with a target. This development of trust is the reason that advocates should meet with elected officials and their staffs in order to develop connections and establish a relationship *before* a legislative session (Ezell, 2001; Hoefer, 2001; Richan, 1996; Schneider & Lester, 2001). Developing trust early will make the advocate's job much easier later on, when in the midst of voting no time is available to make a persuasive pitch on a bill or issue.

Trustworthiness may also be enhanced if one counteracts two particular types of bias that your audience may infer about you: knowledge bias and reporting bias (Perloff, 1993).

Audiences often attribute a bias to speakers and other persuaders. If, for example, you are a social worker, most listeners will expect you to be in favor of more spending on social services. If you are a minority female, most will expect you to be in favor of affirmative action and equal pay for women. Knowledge bias is when the audience "assumes that [the speaker's] background (gender, ethnicity, age) and knowledge about the topic [prevent] them from looking objectively at the various sides of the issue" (Perloff, 1993, p. 143). It is difficult to be persuasive in these circumstances if you fulfill your audience's preconceptions. If, on the other hand, you speak against the expected bias, you have increased trustworthiness. You have become a "convert communicator" (Levine & Valle, 1975). Just as Richard Nixon, the hard-line anti-Communist president, was able to open diplomatic doors to Red China and not be accused of being soft on Communism, people who take the side of an argument that is the opposite of what is expected gain credibility. They are presumed to have overcome their natural biases in order to look at the situation objectively. It is important that these views appear to be voluntarily expressed rather than coerced. American prisoners of war making statements that are negative about the United States, for example, are not given much credence.

A reporting bias is the audience's assumption that situational pressures sometimes force a speaker to compromise her willingness to be open and honest (Perloff, 1993). People also assume that speakers say what the audience wants to hear—so if a political candidate promises the American Association of Retired People that he is in favor of increased Social Security benefits, his statement is discounted and disbelieved. On the other hand, if a speaker tells an audience something it likely does not want to hear, the speaker's credibility is increased, even if his popularity is not. Credibility increases even more with third-party observers, who later hear about the content of the statements and the makeup of the audience.

For an example of knowledge and reporting biases, we turn to an incident involving Bill Cosby. African American comedian and Ph.D. Bill Cosby made remarks that were critical of black youth's behavior in today's society at a celebration of the fiftieth anniversary of the *Brown v. Topeka Board of Education* Supreme Court decision. (This court case made educational segregation illegal.) Cosby said that African American youngsters were growing up not knowing how to speak correctly and were making poor choices about their lives, such as not getting a good education and having children when too young. These comments were surprising and were counter to both knowledge and reporting biases. A successful African American, speaking to a largely

African American audience, is not expected to make such statements. Although Dr. Cosby was criticized by some for potentially providing ammunition to racists, most commentators praised his honesty and willingness to tell it like it is even if it was not a popular viewpoint.

Trustworthiness can also be reflected in what speakers wear, how they speak, and how they use body language. Clothing, of course, can be used to show authority. Almost all male politicians and businessmen use the "power suit," dark blue cloth with red tie and black shoes, to show they are serious and wise. Women's "dress for success" clothing styles change more frequently but exist as well. Because authority can be used to impel change, most traditional persuaders use some variation of these outfits in formal settings. Clothing, however, can be used to promote a feeling of similarity rather than authority. Advocates may purposely dress differently than when going to the office when entering a community group composed of lower-income or blue-collar workers. In this case, it is important not to wear more formal attire that may send a message of class or social separateness.

The way one speaks can also have an impact on how trustworthy one appears to be. It is useful to "control your tone of voice, speed of delivery, pitch, and volume to project confidence and authority" (Mills, 2000, p.70). Pausing in the right spot also increases the impact of what you say next (Mills).

Body language is another powerful nonverbal cue and a way to increase your influence. Mirroring your target's posture, if not over-done, creates a connection and improves your target's perception of your trustworthiness (Mills, 2000). Direct practice social workers are taught to mirror posture to improve rapport with clients—it has the same impact on influence targets.

Likeability, although perhaps not as important as expertise and trustworthiness, nonetheless influences your persuasiveness. Roger Ailes, who has advised U.S. presidents on successful presentation of their messages, gives the following advice:

> If you could master one element of personal communications that is more powerful than anything we've discussed, it is the quality of being likeable. I call it the magic bullet, because if your audience likes you, they'll forgive just about everything else you do wrong. If they don't like

you, you can hit every rule right on target and it doesn't matter. (Ailes, 1988, p. 69)

Likeability has four dimensions: similarity, physical attractiveness, praise, and cooperation. Each of these contributes to your ability to persuade, but each of these dimensions, on its own, also has considerable limitations.

People are more persuaded by those who are similar to them than by those who are different, in most cases (Perloff, 1993). Similarity can occur across four dimensions: attitude, morality, background, and appearance, although the first two, attitude and morality, seem most important. When solicitors for a charity on a college campus added the phrase "I'm a student, too" to their requests, donations more than doubled (Aune & Basil, 1994). Relevance and the factual basis of the decision modify the importance of similarity, however.

If a similarity is relevant to the decision, it is more likely to increase your credibility. Knowing that you are a college graduate who grew up in an impoverished neighborhood might make an audience in a low-income area pay close attention to your ideas about the ability of poor children to succeed in college. This same similarity would probably have little effect in persuading people to buy a certain color of shirt. In the first case, your similarity is highly relevant; in the second case, it is irrelevant.

The type of decision that is to be made by the audience can also undermine the importance of similarity. When the decision relies upon facts, an audience may feel that agreeing with someone who is dissimilar shows more credibility, as it reinforces that "facts are facts." If the decision is more emotionally based, however, more similarity is seen as desirable for maximum persuasion potential (Perloff, 1993). Thus, the advocate's decision to emphasize expertise or similarity depends on "the context, the persuader's goals, and a message recipient's attitudes about the issue" (Perloff, p. 149).

Most evidence supports the view that physically attractive people are more persuasive than average or below-average looking people (Perloff, 1993). For example, good-looking fund-raisers for the American Heart Association generated nearly twice as many donations as did other fund-raisers (Reingen & Kernan, 1993). Still, there are important conditions that limit this conclusion. This type of persuasion tends to be short-lived and irrelevant to the purpose of the persuasion attempt. Good-looking people are more likely to persuade you to buy a different brand of shampoo, for example, than they are to affect your views on social justice. Also, people tend not to be "attractive" or "unattractive" at all times. One study concluded that slight changes in hairstyle, weight, and clothing would be enough to make the unattractive people attractive, and the reverse (Webster & Driskell, 1983). Although the transformation may not be as complete or dramatic as in movies, where a relatively unattractive person can, by unpinning a bun in her hair, suddenly be beautiful, most people can make changes in how they are perceived without much trouble. This would include wearing a flattering hairstyle, maintaining a healthy weight, and purchasing high-quality clothing.

People are persuaded by people who praise them. And, according to some research, the praise does not even have to be true to generate higher levels of likeability (Cialdini, 2001). To put it bluntly, flattery increases your likeability.

It is easier to like someone who is cooperative than it is to like someone who seems primarily uncooperative. Too many people trying to sell something, whether a product or an idea, increase their target's anxieties rather than reducing them (Bedell, 2000). Following the principles of persuasion correctly will reduce your targets' anxieties about doing as you ask (Bedell). A cooperative approach makes it easy for the audience to accept your offer. For example, offer to help solve problems, rather than bringing them up without ideas for solving them. You can offer to assist the decision maker to explore options or research new ideas. Have an upbeat attitude. Do what you can to be a positive influence on people rather than having a negative, or even neutral, effect. All of these steps will affect your likeability.

In summary, the most important attribute that a message sender must have to be persuasive is credibility. Credibility is comprised of several components: expertise, trustworthiness, and likeability. Likeability, in turn, is comprised of similarity, physical attractiveness, praise, and cooperation. Each of these factors or dimensions can be altered to at least some degree and can be important to an advocate's persuasiveness.

The Receiver

The receiver is the last of the four main variables in determining the approach and success of any persuasion effort. Successful advocacy requires different approaches to different types of audiences. The bottom line of persuasion is a bit counterintuitive, however—you, the advocate, do not persuade the target. The only way a target can be convinced to adopt a view or take an action is if the target convinces him- or herself. Your job as an advocate is to understand the target well enough that you assist in this process. Thus, it is vitally important for you to both gather as much information about the target as you can before the persuasion attempt and be able to change tactics on the fly if your efforts are not working. The only true way to get what you want from people is for them to believe it is in their best interest to agree with you. "People will do what you ask only if they believe they'll fulfill their own personal needs by doing so" (Bedell, 2000, p. 22).

Three personal needs stand out: the need to win, the need for security, and the need for acceptance (Bedell, 2000, p. 25). The first step in persuasion is to use your social work skills to decide which of these needs seems most important to the target. The next step is to frame your communications to allow the target to persuade her- or himself that this need is being met. With politicians, the need to win is usually very strong—they are, after all, always in contests where there are winners and losers. If their need to win were not strong, they probably would be in a different line of work. Still, the personal need for security and acceptance should not be ruled out in any particular circumstance.

These personal needs are strongly influenced by another characteristic of the target: how much he or she cares about this particular issue. Targets who are not particularly interested in the issue may employ "heuristic thought." This type of thought is a state of mind that is not so alert, where the situation is not receiving much attention (Chaiken, Liberman, & Eagly, 1989). If your target is in this mode of thought, it is easier to convince him or her of your position. It is not necessarily the best argument that wins, but rather the personal characteristics of the sender that convince. Easy-to-digest information that looks good and comes from a nice-looking, pleasant person can be convincing if the target does not care much and pays relatively little attention to the presentation.

Although it might seem easy to overturn a decision based on such a presentation, once a commitment is made to support a position (yours or your opponent's), it can be difficult to get decision makers to flip-flop on the issue, as they prize being able to show a consistent pattern of support either for or against a policy position.

The other type of thinking, called "systematic thinking," is employed when a person finds the topic interesting, understands what is at stake, and/or has a strong personal stake in the outcome of the decision (Chaiken et al., 1989). In systematic thinking, the mind is alert and carefully examining the issue. The best way to deal with a systematic thinker is with strong facts and logical arguments.

If you find yourself trying to persuade someone using heuristic thinking, you can try to persuade him with cues, such as "everybody else is doing it," "authorities say it is the best idea," and "it's the same thing you did before." The other approach is to try to shift him or her into systematic thinking by finding a way to show how the topic is interesting or how he or she will be affected by it. The advocate trying to shift the receiver's thinking mode can also make sure that the information is understandable.

Research indicates that if the persuader uses arguments with someone who is thinking heuristically, the process is bound to fail. Similarly, using cues with someone who is thinking systematically is also ineffective (Booth-Butterfield, 1996). Thus, an advocate must match the style of persuasion with the characteristics of the receiver. Although we would like to believe that decision maters give all issues considerable attention and always apply systematic thought, experience teaches us otherwise. An underappreciated reason for this seeming negligence is that, with many issues, good arguments exist on both sides. Thus, a decision maker may not use heuristic thinking because he or she is lazy, but rather because he or she is a victim of information overload and is seeking a way out of a situation in which systematic thinking will not yield a clear answer. A fully prepared advocate realizes this fact and can make the necessary shifts in persuasion tactics quickly.

The receiver can also be categorized as either the "active ally," the "committed opponent," the "uninvolved" or the "ambivalent" (Richan, 1996). Each category requires a different approach.

Although the advocate does not need to persuade the active ally of the merits of the position, the advocate does need to keep the ally active and try to prevent other issues from taking a higher place in the ally's mind. Advocates also need to keep their allies supplied with the latest information to support the cause and to combat attacks.

Committed opponents are unlikely to change their minds, no matter what you do. The usual approach is to leave them alone, as you do not want to stir them to any more action than they are already taking. When an advocate debates or otherwise encounters opponents in a public setting, the goal is not to alter the opponent's position, but rather to convince people in the audience. These people may be either uninvolved or ambivalent, so use tactics appropriate for them, as discussed next.

People who are uninvolved usually see no relationship between the issue and themselves. Thus, the most important way to get someone involved is to show how the decision at hand will affect him or her. If an advocate can link the issue to a strong interest or personal need of the uninvolved person, then the advocate has created a foundation that can be built upon. A novel presentation of the "same old" information can also lead to involvement. We have all heard, for example, that the destruction of the rain forest is bad for the environment, but it is hard to get many people worked up about an issue happening far away with very gradual consequences. A demonstration of how much oxygen a typical rainforest tree creates in one day (by showing a room with the same number of cubic feet of space that the oxygen from one tree occupies) might make it more real to an uninvolved person. (Chapter 3 includes many ideas about how to change a person's involvement.)

As with the other types of receivers, the advocate must try to understand an ambivalent receiver's beliefs and feelings, or what is keeping the person from taking a stand. There are five questions people ask themselves as they come close to making a decision:

1. But what about the options I'm giving up?
2. Am I making a mistake by agreeing with you?
3. How will I explain my decision to others?
4. Am I going to come out of this a loser?
5. Is this going to cost too much? (Bedell 2000, p. 80).

These questions reflect reluctance to agree with someone they believe is trying to sell them something. Furthermore, each one of the questions relates to one of the three personal needs discussed earlier: the need to win, the need for security, and the need for acceptance. If you can diagnose which questions are not yet answered to the receiver's satisfaction, you may be able to get the ambivalent person off the fence and onto your team.

CONCLUSION

In this chapter, I have described the basics of negotiation and persuasion, along with implications for their practical use by advocates working at all levels. Armed with this theoretical knowledge, along with the advocacy map created earlier in the planning process, an advocate is now prepared for actual contact with a target. Presenting information is the topic of the next chapter.

Suggested Further Reading

Bedell, G. (2000). *Three steps to yes: The gentle art of getting your way.* New York: Crown Business

This book adopts the view that having the best idea is not enough—you must be able to persuade others that it is the best idea. Further, if you are correct, everyone will benefit by adopting your idea. Thus, it is a moral responsibility to be persuasive. This is an easy-to-read popularization of the research literature, with many examples from both business and the author's personal life. One of the keys to ethical persuasion is to keep the target's needs foremost in the negotiation and influence process. By following the twenty-one persuasion tactics described in this book, advocates can become more persuasive and more effective in their work.

Cialdini, R. (2000). *Influence: Science and practice* (4th ed.). Boston: Allyn & Bacon.

The study of what motivates people to do something that is not their idea has progressed greatly. This book presents what researchers and professional persuaders (such as salespeople, fund-raisers, and advertisers) know will increase the odds of getting people to be influenced. This book is comprehensive in covering the literature yet also has enough anecdotes applying the material that the reading is not too heavy. Advocates for social justice will find a great wealth of detail on how to negotiate with and persuade decision makers to adopt their positions.

Chapter 7

PRESENTING YOUR
INFORMATION EFFECTIVELY

"Grasp the subject, the words will follow." —Cato the Elder

The title of this chapter is composed of three key words: *presenting*, *information*, and *effectively*. Advocacy occurs at the point when you present information. The purpose of this chapter is to help you learn to effectively present information. Up to now, the information I have presented in this book has been about understanding and planning for advocacy practice, but not really about *doing* advocacy. Without a doubt, all that has come before is needed to advocate effectively. Still, at this point you should be chomping at the bit to actually *do* something and make a difference. This chapter describes the types of information to present and the most effective ways to present it.

INFORMATION

If you have been following the advocacy practice model developed in this book so far, you have gathered a considerable amount of information that seems germane to your advocacy effort. The information may be as simple as stories about how an agency policy affects clients or as complex as a community needs assessment. You have looked at other actors in the situation and, either formally or informally, reviewed their stances on the subject. Now you must categorize all this information and present it in the most effective way to persuade your target to make the decision or decisions you want. This process of categorization will also help you spot gaps in the information. Before discussing types of information, I want to remind you that you need *useful* information to present, not just a random collection of facts.

In the vocabulary of advocacy, *useful information* is information that helps make your case persuasive to the target. Knowing what makes the information persuasive can be difficult. As noted in the previous chapter, different people have different cognitive styles and thus view the same information in different ways. Also, people may or may not have opinions and values about what to do in cases like the one you are presenting. These factors affect their willingness to negotiate and to be persuaded.

The information that you present, in order to be useful in persuasion and negotiation, can be either substantive or contextual. Substantive information is the set of facts upon which you base your arguments. Contextual information relates to how the situation appears to interested (or potentially interested) others—it is political information, if you will.

Substantive Information

Substantive information relates to what most people would call "the facts of the case." Substantive information can range from singular, compelling anecdotes that are representative of the issue to results of rigorous empirical research. In the middle of that range is midquality substantive information, which can come from official documents, statistical data (such as that from the Census Bureau), testimony from individuals, newspapers and popular magazines, television and radio, and public meetings (Richan, 1996). We can rate the quality of these different sources of information as we do in academic research, but for our purposes, the best information is the information that is most persuasive to the target. Thus, stories of individuals, particularly when self-told, are often the most persuasive information because they have an emotional impact. If an advocate tells a legislative panel how many people in the panel's state do not have health insurance and that those people worry because of this lack, the legislators will probably listen politely. If a person who works full-time and is without insurance describes the same situation from his or her own experience, the legislators are more likely to pay close attention. Someone in such a situation who "plays by the rules" by working and paying taxes has a better chance of capturing attention than an advocate speaking about the problem from a "once-removed" status (i.e., the advocate works with people without insurance but has it him- or herself).

Despite the obvious tendency for an individual's story to be emotionally involving, an advocate should have more than stories to tell. Although a story may be compelling, evidence on the extent and depth of a problem is also extremely important. A few isolated incidents do not necessarily lead to policy change. A mix of information types is the best approach, because there are people who require statistics to be convinced and others who are more convinced by testimony and so on. A mix of information will help everyone to find reason for action in the direction you are advocating. The key is to have what is needed for the target to be convinced and for the convinced target to be able to convince others, if needed.

Contextual Information

Information about the context of a decision can be important to a target. An elected official, for example, may not be persuaded to side with your advocacy effort until you point out that your organization has several hundred loyal members in his district who tend to be single-issue voters on the issue you are advocating. Even if that one bit of information is not enough to be convincing, it will be enough to pique interest. Contextual information in an agency setting may relate to the way other staff members view the situation or how the issue is being discussed "around the water cooler."

One of the advocate's roles is to look for potential allies. Coalition building is an important aspect of an advocate's job. If an advocate can threaten to "expand the scope of conflict" by bringing in currently uninvolved people and groups, it is possible that the target will find it preferable to go along with the advocate's position. One way to expand the scope of conflict is to expose the situation and the lack of adequate response to the media. Just the threat of such publicity can sometimes result in negotiation efforts and results.

PRESENTING THE INFORMATION

Once you have gathered the information, you must decide how to present it to the identified target. The method of presentation is related to the type of advocacy being conducted and the relationship to the target. If you are advocating within your organization for a new approach to helping an individual client, your target is probably your supervisor,

119

and a five-minute, informal conversation with him or her may be all that is needed. If you are seeking a change in legislation and have never operated in the legislative arena before and do not know any legislators or their staffs personally, another approach will work better. Even if your situation is like the first example, follow the steps of the planning process and be prepared. What seems like a simple request to you may contain surprises because there are issues you have not considered. Also, remember that presenting your information to an assistant or an aide is often as good as speaking directly with the ultimate target. If you convince the aide, you have a full-time helper on your side, someone who is with the target much more frequently than you are.

The decision regarding presentation of your information has two key elements. The first relates to the manner of the information and the second to the format of the presentation.

Manner

The important elements to considering the manner of presentation are accuracy, time, message style, content, and clarity.

Accuracy means that the information in your presentation has been carefully checked and is fully reliable. Although you do not have to present all your sources to your target immediately, you must be able to document your facts if they are challenged. Without a firm commitment to accuracy, you will develop a reputation for not being credible. As we saw in chapter 6, if people do not trust you, you will not be an effective advocate. Be sure to document your source(s) for each fact you present.

The second important element is that brevity is usually beneficial. Five minutes of your target's full attention may be all you get, regardless of whether you are meeting in person, making a phone call, or presenting written information. The key points must be presented in this amount of time. If more time is granted to you, of course you should be able to expand upon the topic, but if you have not captured the target's attention and kept it in the first five minutes, the odds of you getting more time right then are not good.

You should choose a message style after analyzing the receiver to whom you will present. If the receiver is one person, analysis is a relatively easy task, assuming you are familiar with that person. In cases of larger audiences (such as at a rally), printed information going to many people, or debate settings, you still need to analyze the audience, but realize that there may be more than one type of receiver. Thus, you may need several different message styles within the same setting in order to reach people where they are. I will discuss five message styles: cues vs. arguments, positive vs. negative, one-shot vs. repetitive exposure, private vs. public, and collaborative vs. confrontational.

In the first message style, cues vs. arguments, you should decide if you are going to assume the person or people in your audience are thinking heuristically or systematically (see chap. 6 to review these thinking styles). Choose to present cues if you believe heuristic thinking will be predominant, and use arguments if you believe that systematic thinking is more common in your audience.

With the positive vs. negative style, you should decide if you are going to emphasize positive or negative appeals. In this context, a positive message means to stress the good things that will result from taking the action the advocate is pushing. A negative message means to call attention to the bad things that will ensue if the desired action is *not* done. Some research suggests that people are more likely to protect themselves from negative events than to push for more positive outcomes (Cialdini, 2000). If this research is true, then a negative message is more persuasive than a positive one.

With the one-shot vs. repetitive style, you should decide the frequency with which you will communicate your message. One-shot efforts are less likely to be effective than repeated ones, but they can still be delivered in more effective or less effective ways. Similarly, although persistent and repetitive messages are usually more effective, they can be more or less effectively done, depending on the content and the layout of the information. Time constraints play a role in this decision, as the amount of time left before a decision is made is crucial to whether you have an opportunity to be repetitive or must rely on giving it your best shot all at once.

With the fourth message style, private vs. public, you must remember that information can be delivered in private or small-group meetings or communications (via individual or small-group conversations or written material such as letters or briefing papers), or it can be presented in a mass appeal (via large meetings, media exposure, or mass mailings). Research indicates that having a personal, private relationship with decision makers (an inside strategy) is more effective than working to influence decision makers indirectly through the use of mass media and other public approaches (Hoefer, 2001). Still, each situation requires a separate decision, because the circumstances are different.

The final style is collaborative vs. confrontational. Although the popular vision of advocacy may include protest marches, picketing, angry words shouted at public hearings, and other in-your-face tactics, advocacy is more often part of a collaborative process than such open confrontations. If advocacy is frequently part of your social work practice, you can see that using confrontational tactics at every opportunity could quickly burn bridges with decision makers whose votes or support you need to achieve your goals. At times, however, confrontation may be required to obtain any movement in the target's position. Remember that confrontation exists on a continuum, with gentle, as well as more forceful, confrontation both being possibilities. Forceful confrontation should not be the first choice, but when it is needed, the advocate should know how to use such a tactic to achieve the maximum effect, while keeping social work ethics in mind. Forceful confrontation, such as picketing and protests, may be needed when the target is unwilling to listen to your position, has employed delaying tactics to keep you from taking action, or has been dishonest. Although sometimes effective in the short run, forceful confrontation also runs the risk of making future contacts and influence much more difficult. Thus, it should be used sparingly and usually with intent of changing who the decision makers involved are.

A general template for the content of any advocacy message has two elements: describe the problem (including how serious it is) and tell what can be done to solve the problem. The content of the message should, of course, be in line with the message style. Try different frames (discussed in chap. 6)—decide which evokes the best response. Do not settle for the first approach that you put together; test the message frame, style, and content before deciding your approach. Be ready to switch to another message style and use different content if one effort begins to lose its punch. Try, however, to keep the same frame—reframing an issue is a long-term process that needs consistency over time in order to be effective.

The degree of content detail you can put into your presentation (whether in-person, on the telephone, or in a written manner) will vary in strict correlation with the amount of time you have to present. In a meeting of five or more minutes, you can probably do a thorough job if you are well prepared. However, in a very brief meeting (going up three floors in an elevator, for example), you may have only one or two sentences for each of these points or you may have to combine important points in one sentence. Here is what you might be able to present in a thirty-second encounter, using a negative message style (emphasizing the negatives of not doing what the advocate wants): "Working families without health insurance are in danger of being driven into poverty by one bad break. More than 180,000 Texas children have lost their CHIP health insurance due to state budget cuts in the last year. Their care will move from being preventive to emergency in nature and cost millions more to taxpayers in the next two years. Vote to restore CHIP funding by voting 'yes' on House Bill 124."

If you wanted to take a positive message style (emphasizing the benefits of doing what the advocate wants) and had only five seconds, you might be able to communicate only the solution and action step: "Vote for health care for children. Vote 'yes' on House Bill 124."

You should be prepared to get your point across in whatever amount of time is available. The construction of the content should not change—just the amount of detail.

The sad truth is that advocacy messages often are unclear. In order to communicate a message clearly, you must deliver the information in language the target can understand, and after receiving the message, the target must know what you want done. Your audience may not agree with you or comply with your wishes, but advocacy cannot be effective if the decision maker does not know what you said or what you want him or her to do. Compare the following two messages. Which one is clearer? Could you do even better?

Message A: "Our program's current policy allows children without tutors to move ahead of others on the waiting list to receive a tutor if they receive failing grades. Our policy thus penalizes students who *keep* struggling and avoid an "F." It rewards students who make *no* effort to keep up in their studies. This has happened twenty-four times in the first two six-week periods. We should reexamine this issue and come up with alternative procedures in the next month."

Message B: "Currently, according to the program policy handbook, Section 4(a)(3), a waiting list is required when sufficient tutors are not available, unless the student on the waiting list has a failing grade. While, on the face of it, there is some merit in the current policy, which has been approved by the ADOPR Commission, a certain amount of injustice also emerges, as many times the child who does not receive a failing grade seems to be trying harder than the student who is jumped to the top of the waiting list. This effort is what enables the student to not get a failing grade, yet, paradoxically, no reward for such effort is evidenced on behalf of the program. All-in-all, two dozen children have been given priority based on getting a failing grade in the first and second six-week grading periods. Don't you think we need to do something to fix this problem?"

Message A is intentionally written to be clearer than message B. The problem statement is sharper and leaves out unnecessary detail. Message A also has a more forceful statement of what should be done and by when. A clear advocacy message tells what is wrong and what can be done to make the situation better.

Format

There are three main formats in which to present information. It can be presented in person (such as at a one-on-one meeting with the target, at a small-group meeting with the target, or at a public hearing), via a telephone call, or in a written form (letter, fax, or E-mail). Each of these options has advantages and disadvantages. You should make the choice based on which approach is most convincing to the target and is practical for you. Still, within each format, more effective and less effective ways of presenting the information exist.

The in-person format is generally considered the most powerful, because there is an immediacy and power in personal communication where feedback can be seen and heard instantaneously, even if such feedback is nonverbal. An in-person advocacy effort also shows the most commitment, because it is the most trouble for the advocate to do.

In-person advocacy can be broken into two types: the first is when you present the information to one or a few people, and the second is when you address a larger audience. While some considerations are applicable in both situations, others are not.

First, I will discuss in-person advocacy involving one or a few recipients and one or a few advocates. In-person visits (either one-on-one with the target or with a small group visiting the target) tend to have the most impact. The advocate(s) and target are able to exchange information and positions, engage in negotiations, and reach agreement more easily and naturally. A person who is experienced, self-confident, and well prepared can usually be effective in a one-on-one meeting. Meeting by oneself with the target may prove daunting, however, if you are lacking even one of these attributes.

A group visit can be advantageous because it shows that more than one person is involved in the advocacy effort. In addition, members of the group can lend support to each other. The information to be presented can be spread out among the group members, easing the preparation burden on each member of the group. Group members must be able to back each other up, however, if someone misses the meeting or forgets some of the points to be made. The disadvantage of a group meeting with the target is the need for greater coordination of the visit. One person, usually the most experienced advocate in the group, should be designated as the leader or "stage manager" for the visit; this person brings consistency to dealing with the unexpected.

Examples of unexpected occurrences during an in-person visit include the target agreeing with your position almost immediately, meaning that the job of convincing can be eliminated and the visit can move to other aspects of the issue; the target shifting to a person other than who the group was expecting to talk with; the meeting being cut short; the target extending the meeting because of his or her interest; someone who holds a different opinion is invited to join the meeting; and being asked questions that the group members are unprepared to answer.

While the in-person format can be powerful, certain dangers exist when using it. One major problem is getting off point. The immediacy and fluidity of the situation allows for the advocate or target to go off on tangents. It is possible to engage in a fascinating conversation with the target and never get around to actually delivering your message. In a more public setting, questions may be raised that are purposely misleading or provocative. The remedy for these situations is to have a plan and to stick to it in a flexible manner. In other words, the advocate cannot come across like a single-minded robot but neither can he or she afford to be distracted from the purpose of the presentation.

Besides losing track of the purpose of the visit or testimony, an even greater danger is saying something regrettable. Even when provoked, people giving information in an in-person format *must* stay in control of their emotions. Particularly when conflict is expected, only advocates who can keep their cool should be allowed to represent the organization or present its views. These high-pressure situations may require special training and experience. Advocates must keep their guard up, even when the target seems to be genuinely friendly and interested, as such a situation might lead to the advocate revealing too much information about negotiating plans and positions.

I will now discuss advocacy situations in which there are many recipients and one or a few advocates. This type of situation can occur at a public hearing or in an even more formal presentation where the advocate is in front of five to five thousand or more people. You still have the advantage of being in person and that of reaching many people and addressing their concerns all at once. But these advantages are also joined with the stress of public speaking and the dangers of erring in front of so many people. The formality of the situation can stifle true dialogue between advocate and target, even if questions and answers are allowed.

Advocating at a public hearing is often necessary. Most city and county governments have meetings where testimony on important issues, ranging from budget issues to zoning cases, is heard. Frequently, three or five minutes are all that are allowed for the advocate to present a case. To an inexperienced speaker, this may seem a long time, but under pressure to talk and be coherent, the time may seem to fly by. Agency boards may also have staff or other advocates present information to them. Depending on the board, this may be a formal presentation or more informal consideration of a proposal given by the advocate. The key to performing well in any public hearing, however, is to have a clear message and to practice many times.

Books on giving an effective presentation are plentiful. Here are a few tips to remember:

1. Vary the pace of your words, using pauses to add dramatic effect and power to what comes next.
2. Stand or sit tall but not rigidly—your posture communicates your level of confidence.
3. Gesture to add emphasis to your words but do not get carried away with it.
4. Visual aids or props can add punch to your presentation.
5. Practice, practice, practice! Do not read from a written document verbatim unless you have a very special quote or figure to get exactly right.
6. Have an excellent beginning and an excellent call to action at the end.
7. Do not exceed your time limit. Present only as much information as you have time for. If you have practiced well, you should be able to speak in a natural voice and manner, present the planned information, and stick to the allotted time. If you go over time in practice, cut details out.
8. Practice answering questions, including both easy questions that you may have planted before the presentation and difficult ones that you would rather not have to answer. Find answers that are positive for your position.
9. Always leave behind written material that reinforces the points you made, and provide your or another spokesperson's contact information so the audience can follow up.

In many cases, presentations are accompanied by a computer-based set of slides, using a program such as PowerPoint. If such a computer program and equipment are available, the advocate can make good use of them. PowerPoint presentations are ideal when used to help structure the information visually; to present data or other information in charts, graphs, and animation; and to appeal to people with visual learning styles.

Although the advantages of such a program are many, the advocate must remember several things when developing slides. First, the speaker must use the presentation and not be captured by it. Too often, presenters turn to the screen and read what is there with their backs to the audience. Another common error is to put too much information on each slide. The most important lesson when putting slides together is that the limited amount of information on each slide should be *simple, big,* and *legible*. Each slide should make *one* point. The point can have an example, a visual, or data to support it, but you should stick to one main idea per slide. Any visuals you use should support the major idea of the slide. Font size on a slide should be at least 24 point for the text and 36 for the title. The typeface should be simple, and the font color should contrast well against the background.

Printouts of the slides should be available to the audience during or after the presentation. Some prefer to hand them out at the same time as the presentation so that audience members can write on them, while others like to have the audience's attention during the presentation and to be able to control the flow of information. This decision is more a personal preference than something that has been shown to be more or less effective.

A telephone call may also carry considerable weight with elected officials and other potential targets, particularly if it would be very difficult for you to make an in-person visit. A telephone call can convey a lot of nonverbal information—including the intensity of your beliefs, the degree of confidence you have in yourself and your material, and the depth of your knowledge—as the person you are talking with can ask you questions and receive immediate answers. A telephone call does not convey as much information about body language as an in-person visit, but some things, such as how relaxed a person is (you or your target) can be determined accurately by voice tone, breathing rate, and other audible clues.

To have a substantive discussion in a telephone call, it is best to set up a specific time and person with whom to talk. The advocate must carefully plan a telephone call, as much as or more so than an in-person visit. Unless the target has been told the timing and nature of the call, he will probably not be well informed about the topic and may not budget time for anything other than a short conversation. When dealing with elected officials, it is likely that you will have to speak with an aide, which, as noted before, is a perfectly acceptable alternative. A telephone call made via an appointment is much like an office visit and should be treated with the same amount of preparation. (In such a situation, be prepared to hear the person on the other end of the phone line typing on a keyboard. More and more, telephone calls are logged into a computer system during the conversation so the office can track constituent opinions.)

Of course, when you are working with someone with whom you have a long-standing relationship or with whom you work closely, more informality is acceptable, and it is more likely that you will not be rushed off the phone.

A telephone call to an elected official's office can also be very brief, particularly if all you want to do is ask the elected official to vote a certain way on a specific piece of legislation. In that case, the conversation may be as follows:

ELECTED OFFICIAL'S AIDE: This is Senator Jones's office.

ADVOCATE: I'd like the Senator to vote "Yes" on SB 104.

ELECTED OFFICIAL'S AIDE: Thank you. I'll make a note of that. Is there anything else I can do for you?

ADVOCATE: No, thank you.

ELECTED OFFICIAL'S AIDE: Thank you. Have a nice day.

In this type of situation, your phone call will likely result in a pencil line on a piece of paper under the "Vote Yes" column heading. It is not likely to be the make-or-break bit of information in a hotly contested legislative battle, but it will be looked at as part of the larger picture. It is much better than nothing and, because it is not difficult or costly to do, can be used to activate others who have not yet been involved in the advocacy effort.

The written document is also a powerful tool for advocates. Information on paper, such as a letter or fax, often takes on more weight simply because it is connected with a material object. It may be shredded at the end of the day, but there is a chance that it will "stick around" and be picked up and read again. If additional information is attached to a short letter, that information may find its way into relevant official documents and speeches. An example of a letter to a legislator is shown in figure 7.1.

It is worth repeating that brevity is important in any written document that you hope to have read. While additional information can be attached or included, the cover letter for such material must be short and to the point. Use your leanest writing style, stating plainly what the situation is and what you would like to see happen, all in the first or second paragraph. Many busy people find themselves looking for the meat of the document immediately; help them out by being as clear and concise as possible. If your primary document is more than two pages long, it is too long, and even two pages can be stretching your target's attention span.

Letters, faxes, and E-mail should always be personalized and customized for the particular individual or group to which they are being presented. Find and use the proper address and salutation for the decision maker, whether it is a local, state, or federal official. If the recipient is not an elected official, but rather a member of the civil service, on a board or commission, or an employee or owner of a business, it is even more important to use the proper street address and salutation. In every case, it is helpful to know the person's views, positions, and/or past actions and to refer to them in order to let the recipient know that you have done your homework. This knowledge increases your credibility with that person immediately. Letters also must be timely and call for specific action on the part of the target.

Letters to state and local officials are often delivered in a few days, and a reply letter also can arrive quickly. Letters to federal officials are currently being irradiated and scanned for security reasons and so may not get to the officials in a timely manner. As a result, faxes and E-mail are being used more often to communicate with federal officials.

FIGURE 7.1 Letter to a Legislator

January 2, 20XX

The Honorable John Cornyn
517 Hart Senate Office Building
Washington, D.C. 20510

Dear Senator Cornyn:

Thank you for your work as a member of the Senate Republican Task Force on Health Care Costs and the Uninsured. It is heartening to know that you are interested in one of the most important domestic issues facing America today. I could not agree with you more when you say, ". . . there are many. . . Americans who are uninsured not out of choice, but because they lack the economic means." It is important to ensure adequate health care for all.

The plan put forward by your task force has some good points, but I must take issue with the recommendation to make drugs more affordable only by "extending the federal 340B discount pricing program to additional providers, and freeing eligible providers to use multiple pharmacies." I would like to ask you to consider lowering the cost of prescription drugs by allowing people to buy from the least expensive sources—often in Canada. Canadians have a strong interest in keeping their prescription drugs safe, just as we do. It is difficult to accept the FDA's assertion that Canadian drugs are not safe.

My mother-in-law, as an example, has priced drugs that she needs to take monthly at about 40 percent less if she ordered them from a Canadian mail order sales outlet. She does not buy them, however, as she is concerned about violating the law. She is not the only person in Texas and across the country incurring substantial costs each month that could be alleviated by making this one change.

Thank you for your consideration.

Sincerely,

[YOUR SIGNATURE]

[YOUR ADDRESS, CITY, ZIP–THIS IS REQUIRED]

___

Faxes have perhaps become less used now that E-mail has become almost universally available, but they still have their own advantages. First, because a fax is essentially a letter transmitted over a phone line, anything that could be in a letter can be in a fax. Thus, it is possible to employ more impressive visuals than with E-mail. Although E-mail can have attached documents containing visuals, most E-mail writers avoid unsolicited attachments, because they know that many recipients will not open attachments for fear that they might contain a computer virus or worm. The main difficulty with faxes is that one must be able to connect one phone line to another, and fax machine phone lines may frequently be busy.

Some research suggests that E-mail does not currently receive the same weight as do other forms of communication from constituents. Elected officials apparently believe that sending an E-mail is not as valid a showing of interest and concern about an issue as are visits, phone calls, letters, and faxes.

E-mail is easy to send, and almost every government official has an E-mail address that can be accessed. If you do not know the E-mail address you want at a state level, the Web site http://www.statelocal gov.net/index.cfm has links to more than 9,650 government Web sites at the state and local levels. For the United States Senate, an address can be located at www.senate.gov. The House of Representatives' Web site (www.house.gov) makes it easier to send an E-mail from its main Web site than it does to find representatives' addresses, but it is possible to look up such information. Company and nonprofit Web sites often have E-mail addresses listed so that they can be contacted. Despite the ease of sending E-mail, any E-mail that is sent should be as carefully composed as a letter or prepared presentation.

No matter what type of written document you use, it is also vital to include your contact information so the target can follow up. Envelopes and fax cover sheets are frequently discarded, so advocates should remember to place their full name, address, phone number, and/or E-mail address at the end of every written communication, even E-mail. If the comments and information have struck the target's nerve and he or she wants to follow up, it should be easy for him or her to contact the advocate. More than one advocate has been asked to serve on a commission or advisory group after writing a letter about an issue. Be prepared to follow up on your own suggestions.

All letters and other written documents should be checked and rechecked for correct spelling, proper grammar, and clear writing. It is beneficial if more than one person looks over the document. Several drafts may be required before the wording is just right.

The advocate should always leave a written document behind when making an in-person visit to elected officials and should write a thank-you letter after the visit. This letter is another opportunity to present your case. In more informal settings, such as dealing with your colleagues or supervisor, a follow-up E-mail describing your view of the meeting's outcomes can be substituted.

Increasingly, people are using Web sites to provide information to others. The number of sites grows daily. According to a recent Pew Research Center report, the Internet became an essential part of politics in 2004, with millions of Americans turning to the Web to gather information on candidates and their positions, to read endorsements of candidates by organizations, and to join political discussions and chat groups (Rainie, Cornfield, & Horrigan, 2005). While it is beyond the scope of this book to provide guidance on how to develop and maintain a Web site, I will give some information. Perhaps the most important point is that every major advocacy effort or organization should have a Web site that is frequently updated. Web sites provide information to supporters and people who are curious about the topic. Reporters and others in the media may turn to such sites for background information on an issue. Some advocacy organizations think of their Web site as a library where important background information and links to other organizations are stored for easy access at any time. It is possible to have some parts of the Web site password protected so that only authorized members can see what is there.

There are many other ways to use the written word in advocacy. Foremost among these are sending letters to the editor, writing editorials, and collecting signatures on a petition. None of these tasks is particularly difficult to do but can require time and practice.

Most newspapers select a number of letters sent to them by ordinary citizens to print every day. These letters are short (50 to 250 words or so) and express opinions about current events. Some also respond to other letters that have been published, supporting or refuting their ideas. If a newspaper receives many letters on the same topic, it is more likely to print at least one of the letters. Thus, organizing a campaign to write letters to the local newspaper can increase the chances of a particular viewpoint being printed. Including controversy or humor in the letter also increases its odds of being selected. With letters to the editor, perseverance is important. An advocate may have to write many letters before one is selected. Smaller newspapers tend to print a greater percentage of the letters they receive than do major newspapers, which receive dozens or hundreds of letters each day. Letters to the editor must be signed. If a letter is written on behalf of an organization or coalition, the opinions presented should be stated as the official position of the group.

Editorials are another way to see your position printed in a local newspaper. Most papers offer an opportunity for community or organizational leaders to explain their positions on current issues. If unsolicited by the paper, these writings are much less likely to be printed than are letters to the editor, but editorials provide more space to explain why a position is taken. Most editorials are fairly short, only 500 to 750 words long. They require careful thought and many drafts before you submit them for publication. Advocates with contacts among the newspaper staff may be able to use them to get feedback on their initial writing efforts.

One additional type of document used in advocacy is a petition. A petition is a document that usually presents information on a certain condition and requests the petition recipients to take some action. Organizers of the petition ask people who agree to sign the petition to provide their address to show that they are constituents. At some point, the petitions are presented to decision makers. Petitions not only are valuable in their own right as a way for citizens to express their sentiments, but petition drive organizers can also take the names and addresses provided on the petition and add them to a database of likely supporters of similar future efforts. When writing a petition, organizers should keep the message short, simple, and direct.

It can take a long time to collect names on a petition. Many volunteers are needed to have a substantial number of names on the petition. There is some doubt that elected officials take petitioners very seriously, because they feel that you can get people to sign nearly anything if you are a persuasive person. Still, the effort may be worthwhile if advocates get many names for future advocacy and if the process increases the level of attention paid to the topic by members of the general public, the press, or elected officials.

In the end, the format chosen depends greatly on the way that the target is most easily persuaded. Each format, however, has advantages and disadvantages, and so, if not all are used, the format must be chosen only after careful thought.

CONCLUSION

This chapter has provided information on the best ways to communicate useful information to decision makers. By giving clear messages with up-to-date and powerful information, the ability of advocates to prevail is greatly increased. Attention should be paid to the tradeoffs that need to be made, the methods selected, and the ways in which advocacy is conducted. This is the aspect of advocacy practice that is so exciting—win or lose. By following the information in this chapter, you can be more likely to be in the winners' column.

Suggested Further Reading

Richan, W. (1996). *Lobbying for social change*. New York: Haworth.

This book has extensive material on all aspects of the lobbying process but is especially strong in analyzing an audience. Readers will find more detail on reading the audience and reacting in the most effective ways than in other materials on advocacy.

Hicks, S., & McNutt, J. (2002). Advocacy, activism and the internet. Chicago: Lyceum Books.

Books about the internet are often outdated before they are published but this one provides an invaluable introduction to the uses of web-based technologies to assist in community organization and advocacy. Both a theoretical and a practical book, almost all social workers would learn a great deal about how technology could be used to increase and improve their advocacy efforts by reading this book.

Chapter 8

EVALUATING ADVOCACY

If advocacy for social transformation values both process and out-comes, there must be spaces structured throughout the advocacy to think about and define what success is and how it will be measured in an iterative way. Evaluation, like other moments in advocacy strategies, is an opportunity to generate an empowering process and build capacities. (Clark, 2001, pp. 11-12)

You've done it! The advocacy effort that you envisioned, planned, and implemented is over. Perhaps you met with your supervisor about a client's unmet needs. Maybe you told the board of directors at an agency how the agency's policy was negatively affecting clients and offered ideas for improvement. You might have testified to a legislator's aide about changes to a bill that could benefit many citizens of your state. Whatever your advocacy effort was, you have done it, and you are still alive to tell the tale.

But a question still looms: to what extent did you achieve what you wanted to accomplish when you planned the effort? Sometimes your advocacy effort achieves everything you hoped for. Sometimes it seems to achieve nothing tangible. Most efforts fall somewhere between these two extremes. This chapter presents a way to systematically evaluate your accomplishments, which will show you how far you came and enable you to learn from your efforts.

Evaluation of advocacy efforts is important for one main reason: it allows advocates to judge whether their actions have accomplished anything worthwhile. Second, a thorough evaluation documents what was done and links what was done to what was accomplished. Although every advocacy effort is different in nature and execution, you can draw lessons from each attempt. Synthesizing information from each effort can lead to more effective action in the future. When data demonstrate that change has happened, morale improves and people are more likely to want to advocate in the future. This effect applies to staff and to others who might have been involved in an advocacy effort, such as clients or volunteers.

An additional reason for evaluation applies when the advocacy effort was underwritten by an outside source. The funder wants to know what was done and with what results. Conducting an evaluation allows the person reporting to the funder to provide credible and systematic information. Otherwise, the best information that can be reported is anecdotal and limited. A lack of credible evaluation may jeopardize future funding opportunities from that donor.

Knowing the importance of evaluating advocacy efforts, let us now turn to understanding how to conduct an evaluation. Evaluation of an advocacy effort is divided into two parts that can be called the "monitoring" and the "judgment" phases. Each phase will be covered separately, though the judgment phase can occur only after the monitoring phase.

Before exploring these aspects of evaluation further, we must have a short discussion about terminology. The field of evaluation has a large number of terms that overlap in meaning. For example, some program evaluation authors speak of "formative evaluation" (which is designed to help shape the way a program is designed or administered) while others speak of "process evaluation" when discussing the same idea. "Implementation monitoring" encompasses parts of formative and process evaluation, though the latter two terms are somewhat broader in meaning. All of these can be considered a part of the monitoring phase of an evaluation. Similarly, various terms exist (such as *summative evaluation, outcome evaluation, impact assessment,* and so on) that all relate to the judgment phase of evaluation, as used here. It is important to be familiar with all the terms that might be used, as different authors prefer one label over another, but it is even more important to know where they fit in terms of the two primary functions of the evaluation process, monitoring the effort and judging the results. Examples of useful evaluation texts include Rossi, Lipsey, & Freeman (2004) and Royce, Thyer, Padgett, & Logan (2006).

MONITORING PHASE

The purpose of the monitoring phase of the evaluation is to determine what was done, by who, for whom, and when. This information is crucial. Without knowing what was actually done during the advocacy effort, it is nearly impossible to say with any degree of credibility that the advocacy was responsible for any of the outcomes that ensue. One of the first issues in the monitoring phase is to determine what one should be looking at or measuring in order to assess the level of plan completion.

Monitoring Using the Advocacy Map

The monitoring phase of evaluation is predicated on having a clear idea of what you wanted to do in order to achieve your desired outcomes. This idea is formed by developing an advocacy map (as described in chap. 5) or another set of goals and objectives, though I will assume that an advocacy map as explained in chapter 5 has been created. (The two example advocacy maps from chap. 5 have been reprinted in this chapter as Figs. 8.1 and 8.2) Recall that an advocacy map lists the resources available, the tasks to be completed, and what you want to achieve in the short-, medium-, and long-term from an advocacy effort. Also included on the advocacy map is an ultimate social justice–related outcome for society.

Participants should be able to document the efforts made to accomplish the tasks assigned to them during the implementation of the advocacy plan. Was research conducted? Were applications filled in? Was testimony provided? How often, or to what extent?

Because advocacy efforts must stay flexible and respond to changing conditions and needs, the original advocacy map may not have lasted through the entire process. If you adapt it to meet altered situations, however, you should prepare notes to explain why changes were made and to keep the advocacy map updated so that everyone involved can know what the latest plan is.

Working from the latest advocacy map, those evaluating the advocacy effort can determine what was actually done and why. This stage is one of the most important to learning from advocacy efforts—those trying to learn must have a clear understanding of what was done and

FIGURE 8.1 An Example Advocacy Map

DATE:

Problem/Issue: My client is engaging in risky behavior (unprotected sex and recreational use of marijuana) after school and before her mother gets home from work.

Desired Outcome(s) for Client: My client will not engage in risky behavior (unprotected sex and recreational use of marijuana) after school and before her mother gets home from work.

Ultimate Social Justice–Related Outcome(s) for Society: All children will be in safe situations with nearby adult support.

Resources (col. 1)	Tasks (col. 2)	Short-term Outcomes (col. 3)	Medium-term Outcomes (col. 4)	Long-term Outcomes (col. 5)	Ultimate Social Justice–Related Outcomes for Society (col. 6)
Student Client	• Search for acceptable alternative activities to the current risky behaviors • Research potential consequences of engaging in unprotected sex and recreational use of marijuana • Learn skills of advocacy for self and others	• Student will engage in other activities that do not put her at risk • Student will know negative potential consequences of unprotected sex, effects on later life chances of early pregnancy (for mother and child), and effects of marijuana on self and unborn child	• This student will have no more (or at least reduced) engagement in risky behaviors such as unprotected sex and drug use	• This student will not become pregnant and will discontinue use of all illegal drugs	• All children will be in safe situations with nearby adult support

Resources (col. 1)	Tasks (col. 2)	Short-term Outcomes (col. 3)	Medium-term Outcomes (col. 4)	Long-term Outcomes (col. 5)	Ultimate Social Justice-Related Outcomes for Society (col. 6)
Student Client's Parents	• Search for acceptable alternative activities to the current risky behaviors • Try to arrange situation so that greater supervision of client can be done by a parent or other trusted adult • If the after-school program is considered the best spot for their child, advocate for her to be placed in an appropriate situation (either at school or elsewhere)	• Student will engage in other activities that do not put her at risk • A parent or other trusted adult will be identified to supervise the student each day	• This student will have no more (or at least reduced) engagement in risky behaviors such as unprotected sex and drug use	• This student will not become pregnant and will discontinue use of all illegal drugs	• All children will be in safe situations with nearby adult support

Social Worker	• Search for acceptable alternative activities to the current risky behaviors • If the after-school program is considered the best spot for the client, advocate for client's inclusion in after-school activities program	• Student will engage in other activities that do not put her at risk • Program staff will allow student into program	• This student will have no more (or at least reduced) engagement in risky behaviors such as unprotected sex and drug use	• This student will not become pregnant and will discontinue use of all illegal drugs	• All children will be in safe situations with nearby adult support
Staff running the after-school activities program	• Allow this student into the program • Expand size of program to include all students who would benefit from the program	• Program staff will allow student into program • Program staff will have resources to work with all students who would benefit from the program	• This student will have no more (or at least reduced) engagement in risky behaviors such as unprotected sex and drug use	• This student will not become pregnant and will discontinue use of all illegal drugs • Female students in the program will not become pregnant and will not use illegal drugs	• All children will be in safe situations with nearby adult support

FIGURE 8.2   Example Advocacy Map

Problem/Issue: My client and her family experience hunger regularly at the end of the month when cash runs low, and they have been ruled ineligible for continued assistance because they have received groceries from the emergency food bank three times already this year.

Desired Outcome(s) for Client: My client and her family will have adequate amounts of nutritious food throughout the month.

Ultimate Social Justice–Related Outcome(s) for Society: A society where everyone has adequate amounts of nutritious food.

Resources (col. 1)	Tasks (col. 2)	Short-term Outcomes (col. 3)	Medium-term Outcomes (col. 4)	Long-term Outcomes (col. 5)	Ultimate Social Justice–Related Outcomes for Society (col. 6)
Client and family members	• Research about other sources of resources • Fill in other program applications	• Informed about other resources • Completed applications	• Clients are deemed eligible for food assistance	• Receive adequate amounts of nutritious food • Self-supporting, in terms of food	• A society where everyone has adequate amounts of nutritious food
Social worker	• Provide knowledge of programs to clients • Assist client in program applications	• Client learns about possible programs • Social worker is aware of policies of program and the constraints of the agency	• Clients make choices about how to overcome lack of food	• Client has improved knowledge of system and how to access it appropriately	• A society where everyone has adequate amounts of nutritious food

	• Advocate to emergency relief program to see if family can receive additional food • Push for more adequate funding for food programs	• Social worker knows of need for more funding of program	• Social worker tries to influence policies in other organizations and advocates for larger program budgets	• Advocacy targets learn more about program needs • Agencies receive additional resources for food aid programs	• A society where everyone has adequate amounts of nutritious food
Community programs, such as food banks	• Agencies disclose all rules and procedures for collecting and distributing food	• Programs agree to review rules and procedures to determine if they could be improved	• Within agency constraints, benefits are increased—in any case, benefits are distributed as equitably as possible	• Agencies self-monitor their policies and procedures, putting social justice at the fore	• A society where everyone has adequate amounts of nutritious food
Government programs, such as food stamps	• Advocate pushes legislators and agency to examine laws, rules, and procedures for providing benefits	• Legislators/program staff agree to review rules and procedures	• Within agency constraints, benefits are increased—in any case, they are distributed as equitably as possible	• Agencies self-monitor their policies and procedures, putting social justice at the fore	• A society where everyone has adequate amounts of nutritious food

why. Documenting how these decisions were made is also important. It may be that certain people were the key decision makers in the effort, even if the decision-making process was supposed to be more egalitarian. Was this small group of decision makers necessary, or did it detract from the process for others involved?

It may not be immediately obvious how to collect the information needed to describe the implementation of the advocacy map. I describe the most common approaches to data collection in the next section. It is possible to use more than one of these approaches and is recommended when monitoring the most important aspects of the advocacy effort.

The methods to determine if the planned activities were conducted can be broken into two primary types: direct observation and indirect observation. Direct observation is when the evaluators observe the activity for themselves. If the activity on the advocacy map is that classes will cover a certain curriculum, a direct observation approach is for the evaluator to sit in on the class to determine how often the class met and what was covered. Another advocacy effort might rely on talking to a legislative aide about the importance of changing a particular policy. Again, a direct observation method would be for the evaluator to be a part of that meeting, noting the extent to which the desired material was presented. Direct observation can be a powerful way to collect information, because the evaluator can note much about the situation, how the recipients react to the advocacy activities, and other contextual information. This approach is time consuming and expensive, however, if used to evaluate any but the smallest advocacy effort.

Indirect observation requires the use of proxies to tell the tale. It relies on interviews, surveys, and/or records to provide evidence that the planned activities took place. Advocacy efforts may involve many actors, pursuing a common goal simultaneously in different locations, which makes it impossible for one person to observe directly the activities taking place. In addition, resource constraints may prevent the evaluator from observing most aspects of the process directly.

To use the same examples of activities as were used to illustrate direct observation methods, an indirect way to determine if classes were held would be to ask the targeted participants face-to-face which classes they went to and what was covered in them. It may be that the respondents will remember being in a class but have difficulty describing what was covered. In this case, the activity was performed, but the students' inability to recall the content bodes poorly for achieving the planned outcomes, which rely on students mastering the information presented in class. Instead of a face-to-face interview, an evaluator could conduct a written or telephone survey of former students, collecting information on the same topics. Another approach would be to rely on contemporaneous records collected as the advocacy effort was put into effect (roll-call lists, sign-in sheets, lesson plans, and so on) to determine what was offered and to whom. If the advocacy plan was to meet with a legislative aide, indirect observation techniques could include face-to-face interviews, reports written by those involved after the fact, or surveys of advocacy participants' feelings and thoughts about the effort.

How is this information to be used in practice? Examining figure 8.1, we see that the following tasks were to be accomplished by the student client: search for acceptable alternative activities to the current risky behaviors, research potential consequences of engaging in unprotected sex and recreational use of marijuana, and learn skills of advocacy for self and others. Various options for measurement exist. The client could keep a process log describing where she looked, when, and with what results. Or the evaluator could interview the client to ask what she had learned. The evaluator can use similar measurement approaches for the client's second task. And for the third task, the evaluator can use direct observation—the worker could put the student in a role play situation to evaluate if she had learned how to use advocacy skills.

In many cases, examination of the tasks to be completed shows that the tasks were done, after a fashion, but perhaps not to the extent that was envisioned when the advocacy map was developed. For example, perhaps a task to be completed was the creation of an advisory council and frequent consultation with its members. The monitoring process might show results ranging from, on the one hand, no council being instituted to, on the other hand, the council holding monthly meetings with high attendance rates and considerable discussion that resulted in useful input for the advocacy effort. More likely are findings that the council was created but met rarely and had only desultory conversations that had little impact on the effort. Or, if using the example of the student in figure 8.1 again, the student might have asked her friends about alternative activities but found nothing of interest, said she already knew about the consequences of unprotected sex and so did not do that task, and thought that the training in advocacy skills was sort of stupid and so did not pay much attention to it.

In either case, the evaluator of the advocacy should assign some identifier to the level of task accomplishment. This can be a "grade" (such as A to F) or percentage of accomplishment (0 percent to 100 percent). It is helpful to have more than one person make these assessments whenever possible, with discussion of each person's results culminating in the final assessment.

Monitoring the level of task accomplishment and asking how it was accomplished or what could have resulted in a greater level of accomplishment provides considerable opportunity for learning. The idea is not to find ways to assign blame for lack of implementation but to look for ways to do better the next time.

The final product of this monitoring of advocacy efforts is to know with considerable clarity what tasks happened, to which targets, who did them, and to what extent. Only after this information is gathered can the evaluators appropriately begin to determine if the desired outcomes occurred.

Context Monitoring

Although advocacy monitoring can be completed using indicators from the advocacy map only, other indicators may also be used that relate to the broader context within which advocacy is pursued. Such indicators may not be germane only to the advocacy effort at hand; they may impact future advocacy efforts as well and are thus helpful to track over time. These indicators are shown in figure 8.3. The six suggested categories of context monitoring are monitoring your organization, monitoring your reputation, monitoring your target, monitoring your relationships, monitoring the media, and monitoring public opinion. Although these categories will not fit every advocacy situation, they apply to many and can be important precursors to future success or failure. It may not be wise to win a particular advocacy battle if the long-

FIGURE 8.3   Context Monitoring Indicators

Monitoring Your Organization

Do the concepts of case and cause advocacy seem to be becoming more acceptable to staff in your organization?

Do the concepts of case and cause advocacy seem to be becoming more acceptable to board members of your organization?

Are staff members using their time, continuing education opportunities, and other resources to become more expert in advocacy?

Is advocacy becoming integrated into the organizational culture?

Monitoring Your Reputation

Record the sources and numbers of inquiries that you receive as a result of your work.

Are you getting to the people you wanted to get to?

How and where have they heard of your work?

How accurate are their preconceptions about you and your work?

Are you seen by targets and others as being legitimately involved in the situation?

Monitoring Your Target

Record and observe changes in the rhetoric of your target audience. Keep a file of their statements over time.

What are they saying about you and your campaign?

Are they moving closer to your position, adapting to or adopting any of your language or philosophy?

Monitoring Your Relationships

Record the frequency and content of conversations with external sources and target audiences.

Are you discussing new ideas?

Are you becoming a confidante or a source of information or advice?

Monitoring the Media

Count column inches on your issue and the balance of pro and anti sentiment.

Count the number of mentions for your organization.

Count the number of times you are contacted by representatives of the media to give information for their stories.

Analyze whether media are adopting your language.

Monitoring Public Opinion

Analyze the popular climate through telephone polling or through commissioning surveys.

Count the number of "way-out" negative or positive communications from the public, including hate mail, donations, and so on. Are they increasing or decreasing?

Count the number of volunteers coming to assist the organization. Is it growing or declining?

Adapted and expanded by the author from Laney, M., Scobie, J., & Fraser, A. (2005). *The how and why of advocacy. Guidance Notes 2.1.* London: British Overseas NGOs for Development. Retrieved on May 22, 2005, form http://www.bond.org.uk/pubs/guidance/2.1howwhyadvocacy.pdf Used with permission.

term war is lost due to, for example, public opinion turning against your organization.

The first category is to monitor your organization. One of the primary reasons things are done or not done in most organizations is the organization's culture, which determines how things are "done" or "not done." Advocacy may be one of the things that is "simply not done around here," particularly cause advocacy, in which the target for change is located outside the organization. In order to build a clear mandate for future advocacy, it may be necessary to address internal issues of perceived acceptability and desirability of advocacy.

Because individuals and organizations exist in the real world, it is important to monitor your reputation. Even if advocates feel they have angels on their side, the outside world may have a different idea. As representatives of an organization that must compete for funds, staff, accommodations, friends, and other "goodies" that come from outside the organization, monitoring a good reputation is important. Even individuals must have concern for their reputation. If you acquire a negative reputation, you may be shut out of decision-making processes regardless of your expertise, interest, and other signs of high ability and dedication.

Reputation can be a two-edged sword. An advocate may want to develop a reputation among members of the elite for being hard to work with, while having a high status among oppressed people for being a tough proponent of their causes. Still, this dichotomy can be overdone, making it likely that another advocate or organization will emerge that can work more easily to achieve the same results.

It is also important to monitor your target. Many advocacy efforts are long-term affairs. Targets do not often change their views or positions immediately upon hearing your ideas, especially if the situation you are debating is not a new one. Still, change happens. Stories emerge. Evidence accumulates. Pressures build. Positions evolve. These monitoring efforts help remind advocates of what has changed and can be used to maintain commitment to and energy for the efforts toward social justice.

Relationships are one key to successful advocacy, and therefore you must monitor them as well. Most advocacy relies on using the bonds of existing relationships (individual and organizational) to achieve change. You should, therefore, invest energy in these relationships and not allow them to wither. In addition, advocacy efforts often require building new relationships. New and different people are called upon for their strength, inspiration, knowledge, ideas, skills, and connections. As issues, people, and institutions evolve, targets may also change, which means you will have to create and manage another set of new relationships. You should periodically assess all of these sets of relationships.

You must also monitor the media. If the advocacy effort in question is external to the advocate's organization, the media may get a hold of the story. In fact, you may be the one who alerted them to the situation. If the media react to your pitching them an idea, your advocacy efforts can be greatly facilitated. You can easily count the number of stories and column inches in newspapers and magazines. You can make a rough estimate of the amount of this material that is positive and negative to your position or organization. An important aspect of your relationship with the media is also the number of times you are turned to as a source of information or a viewpoint worth including in a story. Finally, because editorials can be persuasive to readers, if an editorial writer begins to use the same language as you do, it is a sign that the issue is being framed the way you desire. When the media see the situation as you do, the public will be more likely to adopt that viewpoint as well.

Finally, you must monitor public opinion. As noted above, public opinion may be shaped by how an issue is presented in the media. Positive public opinion is very helpful in an advocacy effort, to be sure, but media attention to your viewpoint may also bring out people who are working outside the bounds of rational discourse. Such people may resort to intimidation, threats, and violence. Advocates for causes such as reproductive choice or civil rights for oppressed minorities have found the courage to continue their work in the fact of death threats, bombings, and personal attacks. Not every threat can be guarded against, but advocates should follow common-sense security measures when intense passion animates opponents. The ways suggested to monitor public opinion range from the expensive (polls and surveys) to the free (simply noting the number of letters and donations received, for example).

Once the monitoring phase of the advocacy effort (checking that the tasks described in the advocacy map were carried out and/or checking on the context of the advocacy effort) is complete, the evaluator can move to the next phase, that of judging how well the outcomes were accomplished. It is worth repeating that evaluating an advocacy effort must include a clear monitoring of what occurred. Not much learning about the effectiveness of an effort can be done if it is not clear what was done to achieve the desired outcomes.

JUDGMENT PHASE

In the judgment phase of the advocacy effort we turn to the short-, medium-, and long-term outcomes, as well as the ultimate social justice outcomes, displayed on the advocacy map to determine if they have been achieved. For example, the advocacy map shown in figure 8.1 states that one short-term outcome of the advocacy effort was "Student will engage in other activities (not unprotected sex and recreational use of marijuana) that do not put her at risk." The advocacy map in figure 8.2 lists a long-term outcome of "Client has improved knowledge of system and how to access it appropriately." The judgment phase of an evaluation starts with such outcome statements and uses them to determine what to examine in this phase of the evaluation process.

An important aspect of the judgment process is answering the following question: what is a success? As described in terms of the completion of tasks, the evaluation process may indicate a partial accomplishment of an outcome. The female student in the advocacy map in figure 8.1 may be doing some new things that are not risky (volunteering in a tutoring program for third graders, for example) but also continue smoking marijuana with friends on weekend nights. The food assistance programs in figure 8.2 may have examined their policies and procedures but decided that they are fine the way they are. Are these advocacy outcomes successful? To what extent do the tasks need to be fully accomplished to feel that the overall effort was a success? It has been stressed before that one cannot expect to achieve everything one sets out to do—so this should apply in the judgment of outcomes phase, too. Advocacy is a tool used to move toward social justice, and we should not need to achieve all of our desired outcomes before feeling we have made important progress.

Still, in assessing the worth of any particular advocacy effort, one cannot be too easy, either. A lot of time and other resources go into most advocacy efforts—if these resources could have been used more successfully in different ways, that evaluation should be part of the final judgment. Before the advocacy effort begins, it is useful to try to determine what level of accomplishment will be considered satisfactory, if not ideal. If this level is determined, the final judgment will be easier to make.

Measurement in the Judgment Phase

Measurement approaches in the judgment phase are similar to those I describe in the section on monitoring. Direct and indirect methods can be used, but outcome measurement does have another tool in the arsenal of indirect measurement: standardized instruments. Standardized instruments are measures that have uniform ways to be administered and scored. Because the instrument is administered and scored identically across subjects, the scores can be usefully compared to the norms that have been developed in the process of standardizing the instrument. In other words, when you have the score of an individual with whom you are working, you can compare that score to the scores of many other people who have been administered the instrument in the same way. For example, you may be working with a client who you suspect is using drugs (as in fig. 8.1). If you administer a standardized instrument designed to detect drug use or favorable attitudes toward drug use, you can tell if your client is doing better or worse than the others who have provided answers to the instrument. The Substance Abuse Subtle Screening Inventory (SASSI) is, for example, "a brief and easily administered psychological screening measure that helps identify individuals who have a high probability of having a substance use disorder" (SASSI Institute, n.d.). Separate scales exist for adults and adolescents so that the scores generated can be compared to more comparable subpopulations. Although generally used as a clinical tool, the SASSI might be useful to measure one medium- or long-term outcome on an advocacy map (as in fig. 8.1) as well. The importance of the standardization process is the comparison numbers, which allow the worker to have a basis for judging how well the client is doing. The worker can give the same measure more than once and then also judge if the client is doing better or worse in comparison with herself.

Standardized instruments have two other attributes that are important to measuring outcomes: they have known levels of validity and reliability. Validity means that "the concept we think we are measuring (e.g., depression) is actually what we are measuring rather than some other concept (e.g. anxiety, anger)" (Jordan & Hoefer, 2001, p. 57). Reliability is "the degree to which the same instrument provides a similar score when used repeatedly" (Jordan & Hoefer, p. 60). High levels of validity and reliability are both important in using measures, because it gives us more confidence that what we want to measure is what we are actually measuring, with as little error as possible.

Standardized measures tend to focus on individual or family relationship issues. Many of the issues on which advocacy focuses, however, are measured at a different level—they are community or social problems. Outcome measures that are made up especially for evaluation of a particular advocacy effort (sometimes these are called "ad hoc measures") may be good enough because no standardized measures exist. Another type of measure that can be used to assess advocacy efforts at this larger scale is a "social indicator."

The term *social indicator* has no generally accepted single definition, though most definitions are at least somewhat similar. One definition states, "An indicator is an individual or composite statistic that relates to a basic construct in [a policy field] and is useful in a policy context" (Shavelson, McDonnell, & Oakes, 1991). Not all information is an indicator; "statistics qualify as indicators only if they serve as yardsticks. That is, they must tell a great deal about the entire system by reporting the condition of a few particularly significant features of it" (Shavelson et al.). Examples of social indicators include life expectancy, educational achievement, poverty level, juvenile drug-related arrest rates, and divorce rates.

Social indicators are most useful when looking for progress in long-term or ultimate social justice–related outcomes. In the two example advocacy maps (figs. 8.1 & 8.2), the ultimate social justice–related outcomes deal with all children being in safe situations and everyone having adequate amounts of nutritious food. It may be difficult to find social indicators at the correct level of potential impact. Many indicators, for example, cannot be disaggregated to less than a county or even state level. In these situations, indicators are nearly useless to judge the worth of an advocacy effort unless the anticipated outcomes were also county- or statewide in scope. Changes in indicators at such large levels may be caused by many macro variables, including the unemployment rate, business cycles, and even weather patterns. Thus, it is difficult to link conclusively a smaller scale advocacy effort to shifts in such indicators.

On the other hand, advocacy efforts at the state level should be examined in light of changes in state-level indicators. When advocates work to gain new funding for state programs dealing with health issues, it may be appropriate to link changes in health indicators (such as low-birth weight babies, accessibility of prenatal care, rates of teenage pregnancy, and so on) to advocacy efforts.

The most important element of any advocacy effort evaluation is to match carefully the measures to be used with the outcomes that are expected as a result of the efforts made. The advocacy map is the first and best place to look to answer the question, what should we be seeking information about?

DIFFICULTIES IN EVALUATION

Although conducting a formal evaluation of all advocacy efforts is the "right thing to do" and this chapter has explained how to conduct one, it would be misleading to end without discussing possible difficulties that you may encounter during evaluation. Three main difficulties are finding time and resources to conduct an evaluation, resistance on the part of those being evaluated, and disagreement during the judgment phase.

Finding Time and Resources for Evaluation

People who are advocates are usually something else, too: case manager, agency executive, volunteer, student, and so on. Such advocates have many demands on their time, and advocacy may be only a fairly small part of their lives. Few social workers are full-time advocates, and even those who are have many other tasks to complete. Thus, it is easy to think that evaluation will get done later, after a new project is completed. As the advocacy effort to be evaluated recedes in time, the pressure to evaluate it fades.

Because "time is money," a lack of staff or volunteer time could be ameliorated if more money was provided for evaluation and someone was hired to complete an evaluation. Unfortunately, most advocacy efforts directed at improving social justice are as short of funds as they are of time. So it is difficult to throw money at the problem to make it go away.

This problem can be reduced by using volunteer evaluators, such as those from a local university class or others who are willing to take on such a specialized role. The problem can also be reduced by explicit support from the advocacy effort's leaders who build evaluation into the effort's staffing and budget. Ongoing measurement of the activities and outcomes also assists in keeping the advocacy going in the planned direction; therefore, a well-implemented effort should already have many of the important data collected by the end of the project. Compiling information already in records, while not time or cost free, is also not very expensive. Using the advocacy map helps to make evaluation an integral part of the entire process.

Resistance on the Part of Those Being Evaluated

Few people like to be graded. Not many people like to grade others, either. No matter how often an evaluator repeats, "This is not an evaluation of the people involved; it is an evaluation of how closely we came to achieving our desired outcomes," the people involved feel that they are being personally scrutinized for mistakes they may have made. Few organizations have such a strong learning culture as to be able to avoid this situation and these feelings. Resistance to the idea of a formal evaluation thus arises from personal feelings, even if the expressed problem is something else, such as a lack of time or funds.

At its heart, this problem is nearly impossible to eliminate. The best that can be done is to have strong leadership support for evaluation and to insist that the evaluation is for learning, not punishing. This position is difficult to maintain, however, if clear evidence of bungling or lack of effort emerges. Another element that reduces staff resistance is if the organization's culture embraces improved performance based on feedback, rather than advancement based on mistakes going unnoticed.

Disagreement during the Judgment Phase

One of the most difficult evaluation questions is, what is success? Several people can look at the same information and make different assessments as to whether an advocacy project was successful. When is partial success judged to be good enough? Whose opinion about the level of success will be adopted? People with vested interests and hidden agendas may want to overstate or understate the degree of success. It is almost a given that any one advocacy effort will not achieve everything desired, so this issue also almost always comes up when evaluating advocacy.

The best way to reduce this problem is to agree after the advocacy map is developed but before the advocacy begins as to which level of accomplishment will be labeled which level of success. With this agreement recorded and distributed, the final judgment phase becomes easier. Assessment is made simpler by having an agreement in place before people's reactions are colored by what actually happens.

CONCLUSION

The evaluation of advocacy efforts is essential to learning how to perform advocacy better. In the model used in this book, evaluation is closely linked to planning of advocacy. The advocacy map is used to monitor whether appropriate and needed resources were present and whether the planned tasks were attempted and completed. Only after a reckoning of the level of resources and extent of task completion is made can the evaluator move to examining whether outcomes were achieved and judging how well the advocacy effort's desired outcomes were accomplished.

Evaluators use both direct and indirect approaches to measure what they want to be able to count. Evaluators can observe for themselves or rely on others to observe and report accurately what they see, feel, or think. Standardized instruments and social indicators can also help to determine if desired outcomes have been achieved.

Advocates, like most others, want to do the best job they can but may be leery of actually finding out how well they did. Although it can be difficult to evaluate advocacy efforts, the possibility to learn from past successes and failures is too important to ignore. Advocates must take a position in which their ethical responsibility for growth and choice for all is large enough to risk hearing some bad news about some of what they have done. Only by testing what has been done will we ever know what works, when, and why.

Suggested Further Reading

Clark, C. (2001). *Making change happen: Advocacy and citizen participation.* Washington, DC: Just Associates.

This short publication presents a range of issues around advocacy and has a good section on evaluation of advocacy efforts. The author's description of the need for evaluation of evaluation for organizational learning is especially strong.

Royce, D., Thyer, B., Padgett, D., & Logan, T. (2001). *Program evaluation: An introduction* (3rd ed.). Belmont, CA: Brooks/Cole.

This book presents a good introduction to the field of program evaluation. It clearly explains terms such as *formative, process,* and *outcome evaluation.* It also does an excellent job of describing the issues involved in measurement of what a program is trying to accomplish. Although a reader will have to adapt the ideas to an advocacy setting, this book provides a strong foundation for measuring how well an advocacy effort succeeded.

Chapter 9

ONGOING MONITORING

"...the client advocacy role, which social workers increasingly carry out through legislative lobbying, should be expanded in concept and practice to include monitoring the implementation of social legislation. Monitoring the bureaucracy, the agency of legislative implementation, is a concomitant responsibility to legislative lobbying; it adds a measure of assurance that change sought by legislation will take place." (Bell & Bell, 1982, p. 119)

The framework I present in this book requires social workers to monitor the advocacy situation on an ongoing basis. Even after an advocacy plan has been implemented and the battle seemingly fought, hard-won gains can be lost. Laws may be passed, but implementation may not occur. Implementation may occur but be hamstrung by counter-productive rules, low resource allocations, bureaucratic indifference, and so on. On the other hand, perhaps the legislative battle did not go very well. Advocates may be able to achieve some of their goals by working through the post-legislative policy-making phase. The information in this chapter can help in either situation by ensuring that advocates understand the importance of monitoring.

A key lesson from research on advocacy is that, generally, more gets accomplished when people work together in coalitions or interest groups than when they work on their own (Brown, Ericson, Trotter, Langenegger, & Lewis, 1999). Nowhere is this truer than when monitoring the bureaucracy, for two reasons. First, a great deal of expertise is required to understand the processes and the details involved in bureaucracy. Sometimes, the insertion of just one or two words can make a very large difference in the outcome. Social workers, for example, were excluded from the list of people who could receive reimbursement from certain federal government programs that provide mental health services, unless the social worker was supervised by a psychologist or psychiatrist. The National Association of Social Workers struggled diligently to have two words, *social worker*, along with an appropriate definition of who a social worker is, included in the regulations that defined who could be directly reimbursed for their work. (To see how the current Medicare regulations read, see ex. 9.1.)

Exhibit 9.1 Definition of Clinical Social Worker and Clinical Social Work Services by Centers for Medicare and Medicaid Services

TITLE 42—PUBLIC HEALTH
CHAPTER IV—CENTERS FOR MEDICARE & MEDICAID SERVICES, DEPARTMENT OF HEALTH AND HUMAN SERVICES

PART 410—SUPPLEMENTARY MEDICAL INSURANCE (SMI) BENEFITS— Table of Contents

Subpart B—Medical and Other Health Services

Sec. 410.73 Clinical social worker services.

(a) Definition: clinical social worker. For purposes of this part, a clinical social worker is defined as an individual who—
  (1) Possesses a master's or doctor's degree in social work;
  (2) After obtaining the degree, has performed at least 2 years of supervised clinical social work; and
  (3) Either is licensed or certified as a clinical social worker by the State in which the services are performed or, in the case of an individual in a State that does not provide for licensure or certification as a clinical social worker—
    (i) Is licensed or certified at the highest level of practice provided by the laws of the State in which the services are performed; and
    (ii) Has completed at least 2 years or 3,000 hours of post master's degree supervised clinical social work practice under the supervision of a master's degree level social worker in an appropriate setting such as a hospital, SNF, or clinic.
(b) Covered clinical social worker services. Medicare Part B covers clinical social worker services.
  (1) Definition. "Clinical social worker services" means, except as specified in paragraph (b)(2) of this section, the services of a clinical social worker furnished for the diagnosis and treatment of mental illness that the clinical social worker is legally authorized to perform under State law (or the State regulatory mecha-

nism provided by State law) of the State in which the services are performed. The services must be of a type that would be covered if they were furnished by a physician or as an incident to a physician's professional service and must meet the requirements of this section.

(2) Exception. The following services are not clinical social worker services for purposes of billing Medicare Part B:

    (i) Services furnished by a clinical social worker to an inpatient of a Medicare-participating hospital.

    (ii) Services furnished by a clinical social worker to an inpatient of a Medicare-participating SNF.

    (iii) Services furnished by a clinical social worker to a patient in a Medicare-participating dialysis facility if the services are those required by the conditions for coverage for ESRD facilities under Sec. 405.2163 of this chapter.

(c) Agreement to consult. A clinical social worker must comply with the consultation requirements set forth at Sec. 410.71(f) (reading "clinical psychologist" as "clinical social worker").

(d) Prohibited billing.

    (1) A clinical social worker may not bill Medicare for the services specified in paragraph (b)(2) of this section.

    (2) A clinical social worker or an attending or primary care physician may not bill Medicare or the beneficiary for the consultation that is required under paragraph (c) of this section.

[63 FR 20128, Apr. 23, 1998]

Source: United States Government Printing Office. (2003). Clinical social worker services. *Code of federal regulations, Title 42, Volume 2.* 42CFR410.73.

Compare the definition of *clinical social worker* in the Medicare regulations with the definition of *clinical social worker* in the Civilian Health and Medical Program of the Uniformed Services regulations in exhibit 9.2. What differences do you see? What difference would that make to members of the National Association of Social Workers? This is the type of analysis at which those who try to influence the regulation-writing process must excel.

Second, because monitoring work is extremely detailed and relies on a nuanced understanding of what specific words will result in what outcomes, it is both high stakes and "probably the most boring of the political interventive techniques" (Haynes & Mickelson, 2000, p. 140). Groups, organizations, and coalitions are thus more likely to be able to

Exhibit 9.2   Definition of a Certified Clinical Social Worker by the Civilian Health and Medical Program of the Uniformed Services

---

TITLE 32—NATIONAL DEFENSE
  CHAPTER I—OFFICE OF THE SECRETARY OF DEFENSE (CONTINUED)

PART 199_CIVILIAN HEALTH AND MEDICAL PROGRAM OF THE UNIFORMED SERVICES (CHAMPUS)

Sec. 199.6 Authorized providers.

(F) Certified Clinical Social Worker. A clinical social worker may provide covered services independent of physician referral and supervision, provided the clinical social worker:
  (1) Is licensed or certified as a clinical social worker by the jurisdiction where practicing; or, if the jurisdiction does not provide for licensure or certification of clinical social workers, is certified by a national professional organization offering certification of clinical social workers; and
  (2) Has at least a master's degree in social work from a graduate school of social work accredited by the Council on Social Work Education; and
  (3) Has had a minimum of 2 years or 3,000 hours of post-master's degree supervised clinical social work practice under the supervision of a master's level social worker in an appropriate clinical setting, as determined by the Director, OCHAMPUS, or a designee.

Note: Patients' organic medical problems must receive appropriate concurrent management by a physician.

Source: United States Government Printing Office. (2004). Authorized providers. *Code of federal regulations, Title 32, Volume 2*. 32CFR199.6.

---

conduct monitoring work than are individuals working on their own, because the groups have a continuing presence in the policy arena and can hire expertise, rather than having to learn from experience. No matter how boring the work may seem to some, others find such tasks highly interesting, because they involve promoting social justice in this specialized way. Interest groups with staff, such as the National Association of Social Workers or the Disability Rights Education and Defense Fund, are natural sources for people to monitor the regulation-writing process, as their members have much to gain or lose from the way regulations are written.

All nonprofit organizations, however, are able to monitor the executive side of the policy process and should do so based on their concern for social justice in general or for certain populations. This type of work has become a more important part of what the nonprofit sector does. In fact, "the monitoring and influencing of government may be emerging as one of the single most important and effective functions of the private nonprofit sector" (Commission on Private Philanthropy and Public Needs, 1975, p. 45). Despite the importance of the subject matter, little research has been done to evaluate this prediction.

Two of the earliest social work authors to write about monitoring social policy implementation define the activity of monitoring as "scrutinizing the actions and performances of both public and private social agencies as they implement social legislation" (Bell & Bell, 1982, p. 120). Furthermore,

> this scrutiny includes such activities as reviewing and attempting to influence the direction and content of bureaucratic rules, administrative or legal decisions, program guidelines, and similar matters related to the implementation of social legislation. The aim of this form of monitoring is to protect the interests of clients targeted by the legislation and to ensure that the benefits intended by the legislation are obtained by the target population. (Bell & Bell, p. 120)

Although monitoring the bureaucracy has many different components, three stand out as most important: influencing the way the program rules are written, advocating in the budgetary process, and monitoring program implementation. We will turn to these components after exploring the differences between the legislative and executive branches of government.

DIFFERENCES IN ADVOCACY BETWEEN LEGISLATIVE AND EXECUTIVE BRANCHES

Advocates who do not understand the need to work with people in the executive branch (at whatever level of organization) are missing a large part of the picture. To be interested only in the legislative arena is like convincing a nonprofit agency board of directors to vote to adopt a new policy and then ignoring what the staff of the agency does to follow, or not follow, that policy.

Two key differences exist between trying to influence the legislative branch and trying to influence the executive branch (Wolpe & Levine, 1996). The first difference is that it is frequently more difficult to identify the key decision makers in the executive branch and to reach them. I have stressed how important it is to find the person who can give you what you want, that is, the ultimate target. But because people on the executive side are not elected to their positions, they are not as likely to be known to the public. Civil servants in relatively low-ranking positions may be the most influential people on any given issue. It takes time and persistence to find out who they are and what the most effective ways to influence them are. In addition, their meetings and discussions do not have to be open to the public, and so the formal avenues of input into decision making are limited. This problem is exacerbated by the second difference between the legislative and executive branches—their cultures.

The culture of the legislative branch is "politics—24/7." People who visit legislators and their staff are presumed to want something, and it is no surprise when lobbying occurs. Elected officials try to be responsive to their constituents by listening to their concerns, so paying attention to efforts at persuasion and negotiation is considered all in a day's work. Decisions are driven, in large part, by what is good for the people of the district who are most persuasive, not necessarily by what the "truth" is about what the best policy would be. Legislators look out for their district, if only to maintain a majority of voters in the next election. Workers in the executive branch, on the other hand, generally are there because of their expertise in a particular policy arena. Lobbying based on political argument is not expected in this arena. Civil servants are generally hired because of what they know and are promoted by length of service and higher levels of expertise. If you wish to convince them of your case, you need to bring additional expertise and rational arguments to the table, because knowledge is what is supposed to drive decisions in this branch.

While these comments seem to apply well to governmental systems, they are also appropriate for nonprofit organizations. People on the board of a nonprofit (the organization's policy-making body) are often selected based on who they know and the fund-raising sources to which they are connected. Some are selected because of their personal history with the organization. If you look on an organization's Web site or letterhead, board members' names are often listed. Staff members' names (other than the executive director), however, are frequently not mentioned. If you wanted to know, for example, how to get the local affiliate of a national child mentoring program to change its policy regarding what it does with the children on its waiting list, you might have a hard time finding out what is currently being done and who is able to provide data on what is happening to the unmatched children. If you called the agency phone number and started asking questions about this topic, you might be met with suspicion and questions about why you want the information. If, as an outsider to the organization, you tried to get them to provide more services to the unmatched children, your right to be involved might be questioned or you might be told that the topic is being discussed internally. If you were able to have a conversation with the organization, they would probably mention resource constraints as a reason for not doing more.

This example is not to pick on a particular agency. It is just the nature of working on an advocacy effort that is focused on the executive side of the policy equation. Let us now turn to the three most important types of executive branch advocacy: influencing the regulation-writing process, influencing the budgetary process, and monitoring program implementation.

INFLUENCING THE REGULATION-WRITING PROCESS

Although considerable research on group influence on the legislative branch exists, much less research concerning group influence on the executive branch is available, especially in relationship to the rule-making process. This omission is curious because the importance of understanding how regulations are created is well known. Indeed, "regulatory politics—the struggle for control over the administrative levers of power and policy shaped within government agencies—is central to government activity in the United States" (Harris & Milkis, 1989, p. viii).

Although nonlegislative policy making is a very important aspect of influence over policy, it is still a neglected area of research, especially in social welfare where changes in program rules can have dramatic impacts on individual recipients of aid and services. Changing social welfare regulations without going through the legislative process first became an important way to alter policy during President Reagan's terms of office. Such efforts continue today at the federal level and exist at the state level, too.

A few authors have focused specifically on the need to monitor and advocate program regulations (Albert, 1983; Bell & Bell, 1982; Haynes & Mickelson, 2000; Jansson, 2003). The following four suggested guidelines for improving the effectiveness of monitoring activities are based on years of experience in monitoring bureaucracy:

1. Know the process by which policy is implemented in state government.
2. Develop credibility with legislators and legislative staff.
3. Neutralize the potential resistance and hostility of bureaucrats.
4. Organize and develop linkages with citizen groups. (Bell & Bell, pp. 131-132)

What Is the Regulation-Writing Process?

Regulations, also known as rules, are written as described in the Administrative Procedures Act. The process has been described as consisting of eleven steps (Kerwin, 1994). For this chapter, I condense these steps into three stages (see fig. 9.1). The first stage, "prepublication," sets the process in motion and ends with publication of the draft rule in the *Federal Register*. The agency drafting the rule makes decisions about the legislative authority of the rule, discusses ideas for what might be in the rule, and grants authorization to proceed. Staff members are assigned, and the goal of the regulation is established. The draft rule is developed and reviewed by both internal and external actors. Although much of this stage is seemingly invisible, as with any project, the quality of the preparation has a strong impact on the quality of the results.

The second stage, "post-publication," consists of public participation and taking action on the draft rule. At this stage, the agency decides

FIGURE 9.1   Steps and Stages of the Regulation-Writing Process

Kerwin's Steps	Condensed Stages
1. Origin of rule-making activity	1. Prepublication
2. Origin of individual rule making	
3. Authorization to proceed with rule making	
4. Planning the rule making	
5. Developing the draft rule	
6. Internal review of the draft rule	
7. External review of the draft rule	
8. Revision and publication of a draft rule	
9. Public participation	2. Post-publication
10. Action on the draft rule	
11. Post-rule-making activities	3. Post-adoption

Source: Adapted from Kerwin, C. M. (1994). *Rulemaking: How government agencies write law and make policy* (pp. 76–77). Washington, DC: Congressional Quarterly Press.

how to manage public input, such as choosing between requesting written comments and holding public hearings. After input is received, the agency must read, analyze, and fold it into the proposed rule or refute it. There are many alternative courses of action, ranging from preparing the final rule with no changes from the draft rule, making minor or major changes, abandoning the rule-making effort, and beginning over to the most extreme case, deciding that no rule making will take place at all (Kerwin, 1994).

The final stage of the regulation-writing process, "post-adoption," takes place after the final rule is adopted. Actions that take place in this stage include interpreting vague or unclear portions of the rule, making corrections, responding to petitions for reconsideration of the rule, and preparing for litigation.

What Are the Best Ways to Influence the Regulation-Writing Process?

Hoefer (2000) conducted research regarding the most effective way to influence the regulation-writing process by surveying organizations in Washington, D.C., that were actively trying to influence social welfare program regulations during the Clinton Administration. His results show that the following are significant predictors of a higher level of group influence: having greater access to information from the executive branch, having policy positions that are in line with the administration, using a prepublication strategy (i.e., bringing current regulations to the attention of Congress and the executive branch and offering drafts of desired regulations prior to publication of draft regulations in the *Federal Register*), and devoting more resources to influence efforts. These findings indicate that there is considerable hope for organizations, groups, and coalitions wishing to affect federal social programs' regulations if they understand the pathways and barriers to effective action.

One of the most important findings for advocates is that using a prepublication strategy is very important to being effective. Many groups do not become active until the later stages of the process, once the rules are essentially completed. At this time, it is usually too late for considerable change to occur. Groups that build a coalition and share information before publication of a rule will be the most effective, because they have the greatest opportunities to shape the terms of the discussion by acting in concert and early in the process.

Another implication of this study for social workers is to be prepared with ideas about how to change current or proposed regulations. Being proactive leads to success. This action requires developing networks within the executive branch and reaching out to the persons writing the regulations to discover the issues that they see as likely to be controversial or problematic.

In the American system, there are multiple pathways in policy making, and, in some cases, different agencies within the federal bureaucracy may be assigned the job of writing the regulations that govern the implementation of a law. Human service interest groups should thus try to have the job of writing the regulations they want to influence assigned to a federal agency sympathetic to their cause. Interest groups that influence which staff member of an agency drafts the regulations can anticipate that their ideas will be given a very warm reception by the staff member. This decision is frequently heavily influenced by the congressional committee that developed the legislation, and even by the most influential author of the bill, which implies that a very long-term view of the governmental process must be in place even before potential legislation is discussed with possible sponsors of a bill.

We must also understand the connection between what makes an agency "friendly" and social work lobbying groups' policy positions. The reason that a liberal policy position may have been helpful to effectively influencing the executive branch during Hoefer's (2000) study is that policy positions of the president in office were liberal. The opposite was true during the more conservative administrations of Presidents Ronald Reagan, George H. W. Bush, and George W. Bush. One interest group representative for gay, lesbian, and transgendered individuals indicated that his group had had no access to the regulation-writing civil servants during the elder Bush's years in the White House. In other words, you are more likely to be successful if your policy positions are similar to those of the president in office. Social workers should therefore realize the importance of national electoral politics' influence on what sometimes is seen as an obscure and unimportant element of the policy process, the writing of regulations.

A final implication of Hoefer's (2000) research is that success in influencing social program regulations requires resources, and the more the better. Money is translated into staff and other key resources for making a difference. Social workers, if they are to create a more effective voice for themselves and their clients, must, thus, be willing to devote their funds to supporting the organizations that represent them in the halls of power.

INFLUENCING THE BUDGETARY PROCESS

The budgetary process allocates the primary resource of all programs—money—to the different agencies responsible for implementing programs and to the individual programs within an agency. If a program has gone through the legislative process, has had regulations written for it, and is ready to move forward to provide services, but does not have sufficient resources to serve those who are eligible, something negative has happened. People will wonder why they are not getting the benefits they thought would be available to them. Decision makers who are against the program will make an issue of its limited success, ignoring the reality of the skimpy funding. These reactions may eventually lead to significant cuts in the program's remaining budget or a dismantling of the program altogether. In order to prevent this cycle from occurring, it is important to try to influence the budgetary process.

The budgetary process is both a legislative and an administrative process. Legislative advocacy as I have discussed it elsewhere in the book is applicable in the legislative arena, but administrative budgeting decisions are the topic, now, and advocacy for them is quite different. One of the most important differences between the executive branch and the legislative branch is that information can be more difficult to obtain and to influence in the executive branch than in the legislative branch. This circumstance again shows the importance of having specialized information about the budgetary process and an extensive network of contacts within the agency.

The budgetary process varies from agency to agency. Most governmental agencies are asked to develop a budget that then is adjusted and approved by the top persons in the executive branch, aggregated with the budgets for other agencies, and further adjusted before approval by the legislative branch. The level of discretion may be small once the budget bill is passed for any given agency. In these cases, the best way to influence the budget process is to be involved in setting the agency priorities in the early budgetary discussions. If you want more funding for homeless veterans, for example, you will have to make your case early so that priorities can be reordered in the initial budgetary request.

For many nonprofit agencies, budget processes are highly dependent on what funding sources will pay for. If a grant is obtained for a particular service, that service will be provided. If donors can be motivated to support a program, it will probably continue. Thus, the advocate in this situation may need to work with the agency to find income sources.

In either of these scenarios, the most important element of being persuasive is to have up-to-date and reliable information about the unmet need. Evidence of need, such as the number and percent of children without health insurance, can be found with social indicators. It can also be found in the size of client waiting lists for services, in systematic surveys, or in community needs assessments. Often, government and agency officials do not take the time to look for additional problems to address. They feel that their hands are full already. It is the job of advocates to bring forward such information and to advocate for monetary resources to be allocated to fix the identified problems.

INFLUENCING THE IMPLEMENTATION PROCESS

Implementation is the actual running of a program. Monitoring is vital at this point, because it is when real clients meet real agency workers that the program comes alive. If patterns of discrimination or omission can be observed, it is up to advocates to try to bring attention to these problems and have them rectified.

Up until now in this book, the focus has been on changing policy in a legislative or policy-setting context. Although I have used many examples to show that the same process applies in advocating for individuals, groups, or communities, more of the examples have focused on influencing decision makers who can change policy (laws and rules) than decision makers who work in a policy implementation capacity where following rules laid down by others is the norm.

The public administration literature has a long history of discussing the supposed legislative/executive dichotomy. At its core, the dichotomy states that the legislative branch should make policy and the executive branch merely puts the policies into effect (Wilson, 1887). Subsequent research and theory casts doubt on the degree to which this division is true. Because many laws or other policies that are enacted are ambiguous or vague, those who administer them have considerable latitude in how to proceed. "Street-level bureaucrats" are low-level workers whose jobs give them direct contact with people who are affected by their decisions (Lipsky, 1980). They also have considerable latitude in interpreting laws and rules and a large amount of freedom because they are not directly observable by supervisors who might want to enforce a certain interpretation of the law or rules. A basic tension exists for managers of street-level bureaucrats. On the one hand, managers want to encourage a single way of acting, in order to be fair to all. On the other hand, the situations that street-level bureaucrats encounter often require being able to take into account the individual circumstances of the case, and so, flexibility is a requirement for effective implementation. A simple example is the case of the highway speed limit. The speed limit posted is the law. Radar makes measurement of a car's speed easy and accurate. Why then do most cars speed on many highways throughout the country? Police officers decide independently who to pull over for speeding and, once someone is stopped, whether to issue a ticket or not. Sometimes a police officer will allow drivers to receive only a warning if the driver's powers of persuasion are effective.

Human service workers have similar discretion at times. Different child welfare workers, for example, will make different decisions regarding the removal of children from a home. Different intake workers encourage or discourage individual clients from applying for benefits available from an agency. Social work education stresses learning principles and models of behavior, rather than a cookbook approach to helping clients, because of the need to respond to individuals. "Start with the client" is a basic mantra of social work. This flexible approach means that similar clients will inevitably be treated differently. It is impossible to mandate that clients be treated exactly the same because no two cases are identical. Clients deserve someone taking into account their special circumstances in order to provide them with the best service possible. Effective supervision can assist in ensuring that similar clients are treated similarly. Social workers should always try to use their discretion in a way that benefits clients rather then makes their lives more difficult.

The existence of the street-level bureaucrat phenomenon has an important implication for advocacy. The decisions made by individual workers may have an overt impact on certain categories of people. Monitoring of worker behavior is imperative to ensure that the flexibility inherent in many social service jobs is used to further social justice, not hinder it. The use of formal or informal racial profiling by police departments may, for example, cause African Americans or Hispanics to be stopped anytime they are driving in a predominantly white area. This practice can be fought, but only with appropriate information. In many cases, the first goal of an advocate is to compel an agency to start gathering certain information. If police departments never collect or report information on the race of the people being stopped, it will be impossible to ascertain whether any biased behavior is occurring.

Human service agencies are not immune to such problems, either. For many years, in some Southern states, when African Americans tried to apply for the Aid to Families with Dependent Children program, their applications were denied. The agency staff would report that an "inquiry" was made, but not an application. Because states had to report by race the number of applications that were turned down—but not the race of people who only "inquired" about applying—it did not appear that African Americans were being targeted by discriminatory behavior. Only after considerable effort was made by advocates to uncover the subterfuge was this shameful practice curtailed.

Another type of required monitoring is to spot action that *should* be taken, but is not. An example of such advocacy is provided by the Disability Rights Education and Defense Fund (DREDF) (Cummings, 2004, see ex. 9.3). On August 11, 2004, DREDF sent a letter to the California Department of Education, alleging that the state was not doing its job in overseeing the implementation of the Individuals with Disabilities Education Act and the Americans with Disabilities Act. (See ex. 9.2 for the text of the letter.) The specific issue is that local school districts did not allow school personnel to assist in the administration of insulin to diabetic children. In this letter, the case is made that not all local districts are following the law and that the California Department of Education has a responsibility to ensure that local school districts do follow these federal laws. DREDF presents evidence about the need for insulin injections by diabetic children and the safety of allowing trained, though not licensed, personnel to administer injections. They cite legal precedents and make an explicit statement about how the California Department of Education should fix the problem.

There are several reasons that implementation may be different than what the underlying law states (Haynes & Mickelson, 2000). Of these, we should be especially mindful that agencies usually try to protect their own interests, and these do not always coincide with clients'

EXHIBIT 9.3   Letter from Disability Rights Education and Defense Fund to California Department of Education

VIA CERTIFIED U.S. MAIL
August 11, 2004   Return Receipt Requested
                                                  #7001-1940-0001-4659-1121

Complaint Management and Mediation Unit
California Department of Education
515 L Street, Suite 270
Sacramento, CA 95814

RE: **Direct State Intervention and "Fast Track" Investigation Request**
    All students with Type 1 diabetes attending public schools in school
    districts throughout California

Dear Sir or Madam:

This is a compliance complaint per the California Department of Education ("CDE") Uniform Complaint Procedures based on the need for the CDE to carry out its statutory responsibility to supervise and monitor local educational agency ("LEA") compliance with the Individuals with Disabilities Education Act ("IDEA"), 20 U.S.C.A. § 1412(a)(11)(A) and Section 504 of the Rehabilitation Act of 1973 ("Section 504"). The Disability Rights Education and Defense Fund ("DREDF") is filing this complaint as an interested third party pursuant to Title 5, CCR § 4600(b) on behalf of students with diabetes who attend public schools located throughout the state of California, and who are aggrieved by the failure of the CDE to monitor and enforce their rights to a non-discriminatory and free, appropriate public education. *See also,* Title 5, CCR § 4610(a), (b)(vii) and (c); 4650(a)(ii), (viii)(C) and (E).

    This is also a disability discrimination grievance against the CDE for its failure as a recipient of federal funds to ensure non-discrimination against children with diabetes in California public schools, required by Section 504 and its implementing regulations. *See* 34 CFR § 104.7.

    We are requesting a state directive by the CDE to all school districts in California which sets forth their obligation to administer insulin to children with diabetes in school, so that the parents and children are not left to the unpredictable and unlawful policies of school districts.

DISABILITY RIGHTS EDUCATION & DEFENSE FUND
Main Office: 2212 Sixth Street, Berkeley, CA 94710 • tel: 510.644.2555 [V/TTY] fax: 510.841.8645
Government Affairs: 1730 M Street NW, Suite 801, Washington, DC. 20036 • tel: 202.986.0375
fax: 202.833.2116

Specifically, all across the state there are districts with policies and/or practices that prohibit the provision of assistance with insulin administration by school personnel. As more fully set forth below, these are widespread violations of children's rights under IDEA, related state law provisions, and/or Section 504 and the Americans with Disabilities Act ("ADA").

Diabetes must be managed twenty-four hours a day, seven days a week; and that means careful monitoring of a child's blood glucose levels throughout the school day and, if indicated, administering multiple doses of insulin therapy. Children with diabetes require insulin to be given at regular times each day and many children with diabetes require additional or corrective dosages of insulin during the course of the school day to treat hyperglycemia (high blood glucose), which in the short term can impair cognitive abilities and adversely affect academic performance. Caring for a child's diabetes at school is necessary for the child's immediate safety and critical in preventing long-term complications.

DREDF has been representing children with diabetes for over a decade and continues to find widespread non-compliance by districts that refuse to provide insulin altogether,[1] require that a parent come to school, or insist that it be provided by a nurse in another school or even another school district. As a direct result, the health, safety, welfare and learning opportunities of many children are directly compromised and threatened. DREDF has learned that the CDE has not issued any directives to school districts on this issue (See Attachment B). Moreover, the CDE Complaint Management and Mediation Unit has ignored diabetes-related complaints (See Attachment C).

Under the IDEA, 20 U.S.C. § 1400 *et seq.,* school districts are required to provide a free and appropriate public education ("FAPE") to qualifying students with diabetes, including specially designed instruction and related services which are necessary for special education students to benefit from an education. Under Section 504 and the ADA, students with diabetes are protected against unlawful discrimination based on disability. In general, for students covered by both Section 504 and IDEA, if related aids and services are essential to providing a FAPE, then the school is required to implement them. 34 CFR § 104.33; 34 C.F.R. Pt. 100, App. B.

The definition of related services that must be provided under the IDEA is quite broad. *See Cedar Rapids Community Sch. Dist. v. Garret F.,* 526 U.S. 66 (1999) (holding that, under the IDEA provision for "related services," a school must provide nursing services to a student who requires such services to remain in school). An IDEA violation occurs when access to school at

---

[1] *See* Attachment A, for an example of a district that prohibits administration of insulin by *any* school personnel. Forms used by the San Ramon Valley Unified School District include "Designated Giver of Insulin Injection" with explicit prohibitions such as "cannot be school personnel."

all, and/or placement in the least restrictive environment are compromised by the District's refusal to provide the services necessary. *Id.*

Similarly, under Section 504, such aids have been interpreted to include non-academic aids, like health services. 34 CFR § 104.37. *See also, Culver City (CA) Unified Sch. Dist.,* Complaint No. 09-90-1007 (March 23, 1990), 16 EHLR 673 (administering medications, allowing access to medications by student, and developing emergency procedure were necessary to comply with Section 504).

Under state law interpreting the IDEA, Cal. Ed. Code § 49423 *et seq.* and Title 5, CCR § 3051.12(b)(3)(A), the district must incorporate a properly devised Health Care Plan into a student's IEP when necessary for the student to benefit from special education: "specific continuing specialized physical health care services required in order for the individual to benefit from special education will be included in the [IEP]."

Further, under Section 504, school districts cannot adhere to blanket rules that adversely affect the educational opportunities of a child with a disability without examining the individual needs of that child. *See,* for example, *Conejo Valley (CA) Unified Sch. Dist.,* Complaint No. 09-93-1002 (Oct. 27, 1993), 20 IDELR 1276. In *Conejo Valley,* the Office of Civil Rights, U.S. Department of Education declared that injections of medicine are "a required related aid or service" if they are necessary for a student to effectively participate in an educational program.[2] The OCR also found that "[s]uch services, including the administration of injections by trained lay-persons, are commonly provided by many school districts." *Id.* OCR directed the district to examine each student's needs individually and noted that another school district in the area "provides designated lay personnel to administer injections to diabetic students." *Id.* The district had suggested transferring the student to another school closer to a hospital or to a school with a full-time nurse. The OCR concluded that these suggestions were based on the district's blanket refusal to allow non-licensed personnel to administer injections and not "the individual needs" of the student. According to *Conejo Valley,* a school district cannot rely on a blanket rule to refuse assistance to a diabetic student or to force such a student to transfer. The OCR found that the district, in failing to address the student's individual needs, violated Section 504 regulations, 34 C.F.R. §§ 104.33-4.

The administration of insulin is a procedure that should be performed in the school environment as necessary and can be performed by properly trained and supervised non-licensed personnel. *See* Position Statement by the American Diabetes Association, the largest and most preeminent diabetes

---

[2]Though the OCR's findings were based on Section 504's right to a FAPE and the ADA, the student in *Conejo Valley* had Down Syndrome and was covered by the IDEA as well.

organization in the country: "Care of Children with Diabetes in the School and Day Care Setting" Diabetes Care, Volume 27, Supplement 1, January 2004 (www.diabetes.org). *See also,* Cal. Educ. Code § 49423.5, which explicitly allows non-licensed personnel to be trained to assist with specialized physical health care services that require medically related training. Indeed, lay school personnel provide this type of care all across the country and in some school districts in California.

We look forward to your prompt investigation of this complaint, and request your immediate intervention to secure the rights of children with diabetes who attend California public schools. This is a matter for direct state intervention, investigation and resolution for all of the following reasons:

- The CDE and school districts are engaged in unlawful discrimination in violation of Section 504 of the Rehabilitation Act and the Americans with Disabilities Act (Title 5, CCR § 4650(a)(ii); 34 CFR § 104.7); and
- The CDE and school districts are threatening students' health (Title 5, CCR § 4650(a)(viii)(C)); and
- The CDE and school districts are violating federal law governing special education (Title 5, CCR § 4650(a)(viii)(E)).

Please contact me directly, if you have any questions or concerns. Thank you for your prompt attention to this urgent matter.

Sincerely yours,

Larisa Cummings
Staff Attorney

Enclosures: Attachments A, B and C

cc: Shereen Arent, National Director of Legal Advocacy,
    American Diabetes Association Lisa Murdock,
    Advocacy Director, American Diabetes Association

---

needs. Thus, advocates from inside and outside the organization may be needed to work for social justice. Outside advocates often have more freedom of action than do agency employees, but insiders often have access to information that is required to make a good case. In addition, we should remember that legitimate differences in opinion as to what a law or regulation means could exist.

CONCLUSION

Advocates for social justice must realize that legislation, or policy enactment, is only part of the fight. Follow-up through influencing the writing of regulations, the size and composition of budgets, and the actual implementation of programs is also required. Such monitoring work may not seem as glamorous as working in the legislative arena, but it is just as vital. In most cases, an organization, group, or coalition that can devote considerable attention to the task should coordinate such efforts. Monitoring requires time to develop both expertise and relationships, without which effective advocacy cannot take place.

This chapter has provided specific recommendations for how to be an effective advocate in each of these three areas of follow-up. Recommendations for influencing regulation-writing include being proactive and working to influence the content of regulations before they are printed in the *Federal Register*. In addition, developing a network of contacts within the executive branch, finding common ground with administration officials, and devoting more resources to the effort are all important steps to influence.

Influencing the budget and implementation of policies requires gathering information relating to the unmet need and current outcomes of the program. In both cases, advocates can profit from having friends on the inside of the agency who will provide appropriate and helpful information about internal processes. Without such help, outside advocates will find it very difficult to make an impact.

Suggested Further Reading

Kerwin, C. (1994). *Rulemaking: How government agencies write law and make policy.* Washington, DC: Congressional Quarterly Press.

This book provides a thorough description of the process and theory of the regulation-writing process. It contains essential information for anyone wanting to advocate in this important arena of policy making.

Wolpe, B., & Levin, B. (1996). *Lobbying Congress: How the system works.* Washington, DC: Congressional Quarterly Press.

This book provides an in-depth view of how to lobby Congress, as suggested by its title, but it also provides important information on lobbying the executive branch of government. This book is very hands-on, and readers will be able to apply what it says to their advocacy efforts easily.

Chapter 10

INTEGRATING ADVOCACY PRACTICE INTO YOUR SOCIAL WORK PRACTICE

". . . today's social workers are the heirs of a powerful tradition of social action."

(Haynes & Mickelson, 2000, p. 2)

Advocacy in social work has a long, if not continuous, history. In some ways, it is the beginning point of the profession, and by any measure it is one of the most influential and enduring ideas in social work. By understanding the ideas and practicing the skills presented in this book, anyone can join in the rich history of advocacy for social justice. It is not a tradition that is limited by age, gender, race, or sexual preference—indeed, some of the major victories in advancing social justice have been achieved by people who were considered "too old," "too female," "too minority," or "too gay" to be full-fledged members of society.

This chapter looks at some of the high points in the history of social workers advocating for social justice and closes with suggestions for integrating this type of practice into whatever you do as a social worker.

THE PROGRESSIVE ERA

The history of the social work profession in the United States is usually traced to the Progressive Era of American politics, roughly 1895 to 1920. During this time, Americans experienced several important trends. Industrialization continued to bring people from rural areas to urban areas. Immigration continued to bring people from other countries to the United States. Life for average citizens improved with new roads, better communication systems, and the advent of electricity in homes and businesses. Even basic necessities, such as food and housing, were improving for vast numbers of people.

During this time, government—often derided as little more than a "jobs program" filled with friends, family members, and cronies of elected officials—was being reformed to eliminate many of the worst abuses of the spoils system. Direct democracy was creating and institutionalizing the way laws were passed, as initiatives and referenda voted on in general elections were just being introduced as ways to enact a law. Direct democracy was also changing who served in the government, with direct elections of U.S. senators beginning with the Seventeenth Amendment in 1914 and recall elections being allowed in many places.

Amidst these conditions and changes, poverty and need continued. Two approaches were developed to alleviate these problems. The Charity Organization Societies were set up to "engage in a careful diagnostic and supervising process, as they screened, aided and finally discharged poor people who needed assistance" (Jansson, 2001, p. 157). This charity work became, in time, institutionalized as casework, a method central to the social work profession even today. Mary Richmond, who wrote the classic book, *Social Diagnosis*, on this technique, was one of the primary leaders of this approach to the new profession of social work.

The other approach, the settlement house movement, brought a different perspective to the table: "Settlement staff tended to be somewhat more reform-oriented, more inclined to decrease the personal distance between paid staff and neighborhood residents, and less convinced that helping could be reduced to a science" (Jansson, 2001, p. 158).

Jane Addams, the cofounder of Hull House in Chicago, is considered one of the most famous proponents of this view of fighting social problems. Progressives fought hard to establish the principle that government could be used to combat social problems and be a force for uplifting its citizens. Issues involving women and children came to the forefront of public attention, and government-based solutions were adopted. The U.S. Children's Bureau was established in 1912, initially headed by Julia Lathrop from Hull House, in Chicago. States began programs called widows' pensions (Missouri was the first, in 1911) that provided financial assistance to single mothers whose husbands had died. Other topics of advocacy during this time period were promoting women's right to vote and civil rights for African Americans. School social work started with "visiting teachers" who went to children's houses to work with their parents on various problems.

Additional advocates during this time period included Jeannette Rankin, a social worker and the first woman elected to Congress. She introduced a bill in 1918 that—when later passed in 1921, after Rankin was no longer in Congress—made available funds for local health authorities to provide maternal and infant health services. Florence Kelly and other settlement house workers advocated diligently to reform child labor laws, and a law was passed in 1916 that eliminated many forms of child labor.

From the beginning of the profession's existence, then, social workers have been involved in advocacy for increased social justice. Shortly after the Progressive Era, however, concerns over professionalization and wanting to shed the stigma of working with the poor took hold of social workers. The next era of significant advocacy by social workers began with the Great Depression of the 1930s.

THE GREAT DEPRESSION AND THE NEW DEAL

The nascent profession of social work turned away from large-scale advocacy during Word War I and throughout the 1920s, pursuing legitimacy through the adoption of psychoanalytic techniques pioneered by psychiatrists such as Sigmund Freud. Also new during the 1920s were opportunities for college-based education in social work at places such as Smith College and Columbia University in New York. These concerns took away most of the impetus for advocacy from social workers, although prior reforms such as the Children's Bureau and mothers' (formerly widows') pensions continued.

The widespread devastation caused by economic collapse shook some social work leaders out of their desire to focus on casework and professionalization issues. Bertha Reynolds, director of the Smith College of Psychiatric Social Work, stated that focusing on emotional problems was absurd when so many people were going hungry (Huff, 2002). Lobbying by social work groups, such as the American Association of Social Workers, at the U.S. Senate attempted to make clear the extent of hunger and the need for government action. Unfortunately, little was done during Herbert Hoover's presidency.

With his election in 1932, however, Franklin Delano Roosevelt brought a new attitude about government to the White House. While governor of New York, FDR had established many social programs aimed to provide relief to the unemployed. Social workers such as Harry Hopkins and Frances Perkins were a part of his team in Albany, New York. When Roosevelt became president, they went with him. Even FDR's wife, Eleanor Roosevelt, had been a settlement house worker. At perhaps no other time were so many social workers involved at the top levels of government, advocating for and running programs that assisted a large portion of the American population. Indeed, Harry Hopkins, director of the Federal Emergency Relief Administration, and Frances Perkins, secretary of labor, were instrumental in crafting the Social Security Act of 1935, the foundation for the social welfare system in the United States.

Although Roosevelt's programs, collectively known as the New Deal, assisted millions of Americans, only the massive spending and recruitment of men into the armed forces during World War II really ended the Depression. After the war, government programs providing veterans with opportunities for education and housing helped set the stage for a time of prosperity. International concerns, such as the Cold War with the Soviet Union and actual fighting in Korea, took over much of the political spotlight. It was not until the 1960s that social work became an activist profession again.

THE 1960S: WAR ON POVERTY
AND THE GREAT SOCIETY

Although the 1950s are a time hazed over by memories of poodle skirts, increasing living standards, and prosperity, facts often contradict the idealized images we now hold of that era. Social conditions for minorities and rural people of all races did not keep pace with improvements in newly developed suburbs. Educational inequality was exposed by the 1954 *Brown v. Topeka Board of Education* case in which the Supreme Court determined that separate schools for blacks were inherently unequal. Civil rights groups were organizing across the land. Women, many of whom had worked successfully in the military and in industrial and other jobs during World War II, now were encouraged to stay home and raise families. By the start of the 1960s, poverty was back in the media spotlight. Robert Kennedy had traveled through Appalachia while campaigning for his brother, John Kennedy, to become president. In addition, Michael Harrington wrote *The Other America*, a detailed exploration of poverty in America, which became a best-seller after its publication in 1962.

As the 1960s moved on, racial tensions and other problems increased. School desegregation had not proven easy at any level, from elementary to university. Voting and other civil rights still were not guaranteed for people of color. Peaceful protests were held in all parts of the country, particularly the South, in order to achieve racial equality. Violence sometimes erupted, and as change was slow, frustrations mounted. Riots sometimes broke out with buildings being burned and stores looted.

At least in part to calm these problems, President Lyndon B. Johnson sought to build on the legacy of President Kennedy's vision for equal civil rights and more support for the disadvantaged of America. Many laws were passed and programs created that promised improvement. The Civil Rights Act of 1964 was an important guarantee of voting rights, desegregated facilities, and fair employment procedures. The Civil Rights Act of 1965, which allowed federal authorities to administer elections directly, strengthened the earlier law and made enforcement easier.

After his election in 1964 by a landslide majority, President Johnson sought legislation to promote his vision of a "Great Society." Medicare, a program to ensure health care for the elderly, and Medicaid, a program to ensure health care for the poor, were two programs that broke new ground in establishing federal government's responsibility to assist Americans in receiving this vital service. Other programs were created to assist local education efforts, provide services to senior citizens, employ youth, make legal advice available to the poor, open medical clinics in low-income areas, and organize neighborhoods and communities. This last goal was implemented by setting up the Office of Economic Opportunity, which oversaw the development of Community Action Agencies.

All of this activity to promote social justice was influenced by social workers and had an influence on the profession. Two social work professors from Columbia University, Richard Cloward and Lloyd Ohlia, laid the groundwork for the Economic Opportunity Act through their earlier work with the Mobilization for Youth program (Schneider & Lester, 2001). This program was developed, with support from the Ford Foundation, to reduce delinquency and crime. Other social workers were active in the civil rights movement and provided leadership in community organizing projects sponsored by various Community Action Agencies. Community organization courses, including material on advocacy, were offered in many social work schools, and graduates of these programs were the staff implementing many of the Great Society's efforts. The Ad Hoc Committee on Advocacy, organized by the National Association of Social Workers, declared that social workers should engage in advocacy practice (Schneider & Lester, 2001).

AFTER THE 1960S: KEEPING HOPE ALIVE

Activism and the use of advocacy in social work have not died since the 1960s, but they have not been as prominent either. Particularly since the election of President Ronald Reagan in 1980, social programs have been under attack and advocacy has focused more on stemming losses than on breaking new ground. Nonetheless, social workers have been important participants in the movements for equal rights for women, people with disabilities, and gay, lesbian, bisexual, and transgendered people, among other causes. Without social work advocates and the skillful use of their knowledge to maintain client services, social programs, and legal rights, the prospects for social justice would be grimmer by far than they currently are.

Research indicates that social workers continue to be at least as active as other professionals (Ezell, 1993). Ezell (2001), Jansson (2003), and Schneider and Lester (2001) have authored books about advocacy at the turn of the millennium. Haynes and Mickelson came out with a new edition of their classic book *Affecting Changes: Social Workers in the Political Arena* in 2002. These are all hopeful signs that social workers will neither forget nor abandon their embrace of advocacy as a vital tool for social justice. Numerous other social work authors have published journal articles extending our knowledge of advocacy and its effective use (Bateman, 1995; Brawley, 1997; Gibelman & Kraft, 1996; Hoefer, 2000; Lynch & Mitchell, 1995; Sunley, 1997).

INTEGRATING ADVOCACY PRACTICE INTO YOUR SOCIAL WORK PRACTICE

At this point, you may wonder where social work advocates find work. Hopefully, the most accurate answer to this question is that social work advocates find work in all areas of the profession. The major thrust of this book is that advocacy, as a problem-solving practice technique with steps similar to other practice techniques, can and should be used in many situations and places. Advocacy is needed in dealing with client problems at micro-, mezzo-, and macrolevels.

Still, some jobs may allow you more time to work on macrolevel advocacy than others. Examples of this type of job include working for a professional organization, such as the National Association of Social Workers, or a state mental health association, as a government relations specialist or lobbyist. (See ex. 10.1 for a position description of a government relations coordinator for a NASW chapter.)

Another job that allows you to spend considerable time working on policy and advocating is being a legislative aide. Legislative aides work for elected officials and frequently become the real experts on certain types of policy for their legislator. Some of their job duties include preparing drafts of bills, monitoring legislation, recommending actions that their legislator should take, and frequently representing their legislator in contacts with lobbyists, constituents, and other legislators and their staff. These jobs require very long hours during legislative sessions and can be quite stressful. You may see an unpleasant side to others in a highly partisan atmosphere where other people's egos are

EXHIBIT 10.1   Job Description for a Government Relations Coordinator

---

NASW/Texas Chapter

Job Opening Announcement

POSITION TITLE: Government Relations Coordinator

Exempt Position: Salary commensurate with experience.

Function: To initiate, organize, and coordinate legislative and political action by Chapter members. The goal of this position is to mobilize and communicate to membership in order to build political power on behalf of NASW membership and their clients.

Basic Duties and Responsibilities

1. Coordinate, activate and involve Chapter membership on legislative and political activity as approved by the Board of Directors and Texas Political Action for Candidate Election Committee (TPACE).
2. Organize members on legislative issues and TPACE endorsed electoral campaigns, targeting key constituents.
3. Organize and coordinate events throughout the state to facilitate interaction and information sharing between members and legislators and/or candidates. Facilitate interaction between legislators and membership on legislative priorities.
4. Produce and distribute timely legislative alerts on an as-needed basis to members and related organizations. Ensure Chapter testimony on key legislative issues.
5. Provide education and training to social workers and social work students on legislative and political action through newsletters, website, house parties, Lobby Days, and other presentations as requested. Assist with production of newsletter/website.
6. Work closely with policy faculty at schools of social work to coordinate student involvement in NASW/Texas legislative initiatives, including speaking at classes and coordinating Student Day at the Legislature.
7. Providing staffing functions to TPACE and NASW/TX selected committees.
8. Work with national PACE staff and national legislative staff on critical federal legislation and federal candidate races.
9. Work toward identification and recruitment of chapter members to run for elective office.
10. Represent NASW/Texas on coalitions as assigned by Executive Director.
11. Keep members informed on all activities.
12. Coordinate sessions and events for state conference and chapter annual leadership meeting.

13. Supervise student interns as directed.
14. Other related duties as assigned by Executive Director.

These statements are intended to describe the general nature and level of work being performed. They are not intended as exhaustive of all responsibilities.

Qualifications: MSW preferred. Demonstrated ability in community organization and political action required. Knowledge of legislative, electoral and political process at the local/state/federal level. Experience in health and human services policy analysis and/or program administration. Basic computer skills, good organizational skills, able to work with high level of independence. Demonstrated ability in public relations, excellent oral and written communication. Experience working with volunteers. Ability to work collaboratively with professionals, administrative staff, committee leaders and chapter members. Strong commitment to membership involvement and membership services. Texas license and NASW membership required.

Physical and Sensory Requirements: Must be willing to travel, be able to work under florescent lighting, able to lift 25 pounds, able to withstand prolonged sitting, standing, ability to manage stress.

Benefits
- Health insurance, including dental, PPO paid for by employer
- Life insurance premium (3%) paid for by employer
- Pension plan (401-K) (6%) paid for by employer
- Flexible work schedule
- Convenient downtown Austin location with free parking and private office
- 2 weeks vacation for first 2 years, plus 11 paid holidays

Used with permission. Hansen, V. (2005). *Job opening announcement.* Austin, TX: National Association of Social Workers, Texas Chapter.

---

large. Most legislative aides are young and are in this position for only a few years. Still, the rewards can be great, particularly if you work for a powerful legislator. By working for social justice in this way, you can have a large impact. You can actually help set policy for thousands, if not millions, of people. It can also be a stepping stone to becoming an elected official yourself, as it was for Hillary Rodham Clinton. (See ex. 10.2 for a job posting for a legislative aide for a state representative in Texas.)

EXHIBIT 10.2 Job Announcement for a Legislative Aide

POSITION AVAILABLE

Legislative Aide for State Representative Helen Giddings

General Description:

Position available for full-time legislative aide for the 79th Legislative Session. It will require daily contact with constituents, elected officials, lobbyists, and other Capitol staff. This person will be responsible for legislative research, correspondence, and analyzing legislation.

Requirements:

Legislative Aide must be familiar with legislative issues. Position requires strong demonstrated writing and effective oral communication skills; strong organizational skills and the ability to meet critical deadlines; the ability to interact with all levels of people and maintain confidentiality; the ability to work effectively with others and maximize available resources. The position requires great flexibility in scheduling as it will be necessary to represent the Representative in various functions; sometimes on short notice; must be familiar with community, organizations and institutions.

LEGISLATIVE SESSION EXPERIENCE REQUIRED.

Salary:

Salary will be commensurate with experience.

Retrieved March 17, 2005, from www.house.state.tx.us/employment/jobs/legAide.htm

---

Sometimes large organizations hire social workers as advocates. One example is a large nonprofit hospital, Children's Medical Center in Dallas, Texas, that employs an advocacy manager. Their Web site lists the following information under the heading "Public Affairs":

> Children don't vote. They must rely on adults and organizations like Children's to be their advocates. Children's takes this charge seriously through a combined effort of legislative, grassroots, and media strategies. The goal is to ensure that children's needs are kept at the forefront of the public policy debate. (Children's Medical Center, n.d.)

My final example of a job that allows a social worker to spend considerable time conducting advocacy for social justice is any elected position. Most people begin their electoral careers at a local level, such as on a school board or city council. This step is often preceded by time spent on appointed committees, such as those at a municipal level, those working to distribute Community Development Block Grant funds, or oversight boards, such as a citizen's police department panel. Other political careers have been started from being a community or neighborhood activist or working within the Parent-Teachers Association. These types of experiences definitely move people from being spectators in politics to being gladiators.

This book provides you with the tools required to become a part of the social work advocacy tradition. You have learned that

advocacy practice is compatible with the generalist practice model of social work taught in many social work programs and follows a parallel set of steps as do other types of social work practice;

social justice is the most important aim of the social work profession and thus of advocacy practice;

advocacy is declared to be something that social workers should do by the National Association of Social Work's Code of Ethics;

the factors that influence whether a person is an advocate or not can be altered to increase the probability that a person will engage in advocacy practice;

understanding an issue is achieved by answering five questions: What is the issue? Who is affected and how? What are the causes of the issue? What are possible solutions to the issue? and How do proposed solutions lead to social justice?

advocacy planning is facilitated by using an advocacy map, which explicitly connects proposed actions with the outcomes desired for the advocacy effort;

advocacy practice often involves the use of negotiation skills, such as setting forth an initial position and various fallback positions and knowing your limit;

advocacy practitioners use skills in persuasion to achieve their desired outcomes. They try to understand the variables of context, message, sender, and receiver to achieve the highest level of persuasive power possible;

presenting useful information in an effective way to your advocacy targets is vital to success. Information can be presented in various ways, and advocates should choose their method carefully for maximum effect;

advocacy efforts should be evaluated to document success and to learn from the experience what was successful and what was less successful. The advocacy map developed in the planning stage is useful in evaluation efforts because it guides the evaluator's monitoring and judgment processes; and

advocates must monitor what happens to the changes they accomplish through policy change—if not, clients may not receive the benefit of what was won through advocacy. Areas of monitoring include the creation of regulations, program budgeting, and program implementation.

This list is a great deal to have covered and to remember. As with all new skills, it takes a willingness to go beyond what you are comfortable doing in order to become adept at using your new knowledge. Several suggestions can help in moving from being an advocacy novice to being an advocacy master:

1. Allow yourself to be nervous as you engage in the process.
2. Try to find a teacher or mentor who can lead you through the process. Your mentor, to be most useful, should already be a master in the art. If there is no one person who has all the skills you wish to learn, find different people who have some of the skills you are looking for.
3. Be open to learning from anyone, but be sure to check his or her suggestions against reality by monitoring your progress on a regular basis.
4. Do not be afraid to make mistakes—it means you are trying something new to improve your skills.
5. Learn from your errors, but try not to make the same ones again.
6. Advocate, advocate, and advocate some more.
7. After you have some experience, teach others what you know. Nothing forces you to deepen your own knowledge and analyze your own practice like teaching someone else.

As you move through your social work career, whether you work primarily with individuals in a direct practice setting, or with groups or communities and whether you work with children, women, the elderly, teens, or other populations, be sure to be an advocacy practitioner. It is on that basis and that basis alone that social work values will become a stronger part of our world.

Suggested Further Reading

Several good descriptions of the history of social policy in the United States and the forces that shaped it are available. All will provide insight into the historical roots of current social policy and the effect of individual and group efforts to make governmental policy more just. Three of the most thorough ones are listed below.

Day, P. (2003). *A new history of social welfare* (4th ed.). Boston: Allyn & Bacon.

Jansson, B. (2004). *The reluctant welfare state: American social welfare policies—past, present, and future* (5th ed.). Belmont, CA: Wadsworth.

Trattner, W. (1998). *From poor law to welfare state* (4th ed.). New York: Free Press.

REFERENCES

Abbott, A. (1988). *Professional choices: Values at work*. Silver Spring, MD: NASW Press.

Ailes, R. (with Kraushar, J.) (1988). *You are the message*. Homewood, IL: Dow Jones-Irwin.

Albert, R. (1983). Social work advocacy in the regulatory process. *Social Casework, 64*(8), 473–481.

Alinsky, S. (1972). *Rules for radicals*. New York: Vintage Books.

Amidei, N. (1987). The new activism picks up steam. *Public Welfare, 45*(3), 21–26.

Aune, R., & Basil, M. (1994). A relational obligations approach to the foot-in-the-mouth effect. *Journal of Applied Social Psychology, 24*(6), 546–556.

Authorized providers. (2004). *Code of federal regulations, Title 32, Volume 2* (32CFR199.6). Washington, DC: U.S. Government Printing Office.

Barker, R. (1995). *The social work dictionary* (3rd ed.). Washington, DC: NASW Press.

Barrett, S. (2001). The dark side of Linus Pauling's legacy. In *Quackwatch*. Retrieved May 24, 2005, from http://www.quackwatch.org/01QuackeryRelated Topics/pauling.html

Bateman, N. (1995). *Advocacy skills: A handbook for human service professionals*. Brookfield, VT: Ashgate Publishing.

Baumgartner, F., & Jones, B. (1993). *Agendas and instability in American politics*. Chicago: University of Chicago Press.

Bedell, G. (2000). *Three steps to yes: The gentle art of getting your way*. New York: Crown Business.

Bell, W., & Bell, B. (1982). Monitoring the bureaucracy: An extension of legislative lobbying. In M. Mahaffey & J. Hanks (Eds.), *Practical politics: Social work and political responsibility* (pp. 118–135). Silver Spring, MD: NASW Press.

Benson, M. (2004, April 11). Tax time renews cries of class warfare. *Austin American Statesman*, pp. E1, E4.

Best, J. (2001). *Damned lies and statistics: Untangling numbers from the media, politicians and activists*. Berkeley, CA: University of California Press.

Booth-Butterfield, S. (1996). *Dual process persuasion*. Retrieved June 28, 2004, from West Virginia University Web site: http://www.as.wvu.edu/~sbb/comm221/chapters/dual.htm

Brady, H., Verba, S., & Schlozman, K. (1995). Beyond SES: A resource model of political participation. *American Political Science Review, 89*(2), 271-294.

Brawley, E. (1997). Teaching social work students to use advocacy skills through the mass media. *Journal of Social Work Education, 33*(3), 445-460.

Briggs, H. E., & Rzepnicki, T. L. (Eds.). (2004). *Using evidence in social work practice: Behavioral perspectives.* Chicago: Lyceum Books.

Brown, L., Ericson, J., Trotter, R., Jr., Langenegger, J., & Lewis, T. (1999). *Practicing Texas politics: A brief survey* (6th ed.). Boston: Houghton Mifflin.

Chaiken, S., Liberman, A., & Eagly, A. (1989). Heuristic and systematic information processing within and beyond the persuasion context. In J. Uleman & J. Bargh (Eds.), *Unintended Thought* (pp. 212-252). New York: Guilford.

Children's Medical Center. (n.d.). *Public affairs.* Retrieved March 17, 2005, from http://www.childrens.com/community/community_public_affairs.cfm?nav=51

Cialdini, R. (2000). *Influence: Science and practice* (4th ed.). Boston: Pearson, Allyn & Bacon.

Cialdini, R. (2001, February). The science of persuasion. *Scientific American, 76-81.*

Clark, C. (2001). *Making change happen: Advocacy and citizen participation.* Washington, DC: Just Associates.

Clinical social worker services. (2003). *Code of federal regulations, Title 42, Volume 2* (42CFR410.73). Washington, DC: U.S. Government Printing Office.

Cohen, W. (1966). What every social worker should know about political action. *Social Work, 11*(4), 7-11.

Cooper, J., Bennett, E., & Sukel, H. (1996). Complex scientific testimony: How do jurors make decisions? *Law and Human Behavior, 20*, 379-394.

Csikai, E., & Rozensky, C. (1997). "Social work idealism" and students' perceived reasons for entering social work. *Journal of Social Work Education, 33*(3), 529-538.

Cummings, L. (2004). *Letter to the California Department of Education.* Retrieved September 9, 2004, from the Disability Rights Education and Defense Fund Web site: http://www.dredf.org/CDE_diab.pdf

Dahl, R. (1961). *Who governs?* New Haven, CT: Yale University Press.

Day, P. (2003). *A new history of social welfare* (4th ed.). Boston: Allyn & Bacon.

Dear, R., & Patti, R. (1981). Legislative advocacy: Seven effective tactics. *Social Work, 26*(4), 289-296.

De Bono, E. (1999). *Six thinking hats.* Boston: Little, Brown.

Donaldson, M., & Donaldson, M. (1996). *Negotiating for dummies.* Foster City, CA: IDG Books.

Dunn, W. (1981). *Public policy analysis: An introduction.* Englewood Cliffs, NJ: Prentice Hall.

Eisenhower, D. (Speaker). (1954). Address recorded for the Republican Lincoln Day Dinners of the Republican State Central, County, and Town Committees of Rhode Island. Dwight D. Eisenhower Library Audiovisual Department. Retrieved June 6, 2005, from http://www.eisenhower.archives.gov/avwebsite/PDF/54text.pdf

Ezell, M. (1991). Administrators as advocates. *Administration in Social Work, 15*(4), 1-18.

Ezell, M. (1993). The political activity of social workers: A post-Reagan update. *Journal of Sociology and Social Welfare, 20*(4), 81-97.

Ezell, M. (1994). Advocacy practice of social workers. *Families in Society: The Journal of Contemporary Human Services, 75*(1), 36-46.

Ezell, M. (2001). *Advocacy in the human services.* Belmont, CA: Brooks/Cole.

Faler, B. (2005, January 15). Election turnout in 2004 was highest since 1968. *The Washington Post*, p. A05.

Flynn, J. (1995). Social justice in social agencies. In R. Edwards (Ed.), *Encyclopedia of Social Work* (19th ed., pp. 2173-2179). Washington, DC: NASW Press.

Gibelman, M., & Kraft, S. (1996). Advocacy as a core agency program: Planning considerations for voluntary human service agencies. *Administration in Social Work, 20*(4), 43-59.

Ginsberg, L. (1988). Social workers and politics: Lessons from practice. *Social Work, 33*(3), 245-247.

Harris, R., & Milkis, S. (1989). *The politics of regulatory change.* New York: Oxford University Press.

Haynes, K., & Mickelson, J. (2000). *Affecting change* (4th ed.). Boston: Allyn & Bacon.

Hoefer, R. (2000). Making a difference: Human service interest group influence on social welfare program regulations. *Journal of Sociology and Social Welfare, 27*(3), 21-38.

Hoefer, R. (2001). Highly effective human services interest groups: Seven key practices. *Journal of Community Practice, 9*(2), 1-14.

Huff, D. (2002). *The social work history station.* Retrieved September 23, 2004, from Boise State University Web site: http://www.idbsu.edu/socwork/dhuff/history/central/core.htm

Jansson, B. (1994). *Social policy: From theory to policy practice* (2nd ed.). Pacific Grove, CA: Brooks/Cole.

Jansson, B. (2001). *The reluctant welfare state* (4th ed.). Belmont, CA: Wadsworth/Thomson Learning.

Jansson, B. (2003). *Becoming an effective policy advocate: From policy practice to social justice* (4th ed.). Pacific Grove, CA: Brooks/Cole.

Jordan, C., & Hoefer, R. (2001). Reliability and validity in quantitative measurement. In B. Thyer (Ed.), *The handbook of social work research* (pp. 53-67). Thousand Oaks, CA: Sage.

Kahneman, D., & Tversky, A. (1990). Prospect theory: An analysis of decision under risk. In P. Moser (Ed.), *Rationality in action: Contemporary approaches* (pp. 140-170). New York: Cambridge University Press.

Karger, H., & Stoesz, D. (2005). *American social welfare policy: A pluralist approach* (4th ed.). Boston: Allyn & Bacon.

Kerwin, C. (1994). *Rulemaking: How government agencies write law and make policy.* Washington, DC: Congressional Quarterly Press.

Kingdon, J. (1995). *Agendas, alternatives and public policies* (2nd ed.). New York: Harper Collins.

Kirst-Ashman, K., & Hull, G., Jr. (2001). *Generalist practice with organizations and communities* (2nd ed.). Belmont, CA: Brooks/Cole.

Laney, M., Scobie, J., & Fraser, A. (2005). *The how and why of advocacy. Guidance* (Notes 2.1). Retrieved May 22, 2005, from http://www.bond.org.uk/pubs/guidance/2.1howwhyadvocacy.pdf

Levine, J., & Valle, R. (1975). The convert as a credible communicator. *Social Behavior and Personality, 3,* 81-90.

Lipsky, M. (1980). *Street-level bureaucracy: Dilemmas of the individual and public service.* New York: Russell Sage Foundation.

Locke, B., Garrison, R., & Winship, J. (1998). *Generalist social work practice: Context, story and partnerships.* Pacific Grove, CA: Brooks/Cole.

Lynch, R., & Mitchell, J. (1995). Justice system advocacy: A must for NASW and the social work community. *Social Work, 40*(1), 9-12.

Mahaffey, M., & Hanks, J. W. (1982). *Practical politics: Social work and political responsibility.* Silver Spring, MD: NASW Press.

Mary, N., Ellano, C., & Newell, J. (1993). Political activism in social work: A study of social work educators. In T. Mizrahi & J. Morrison (Eds.), *Community organization and social administration* (pp. 203-223). New York: Haworth.

Mathews, G. (1982). Social workers and political influence. *Social Service Review, 56*(4), 616-628.

May, P. (1981). Hints for crafting alternative policies. *Policy Analysis, 7*(2), 227-244.

McMahon, M. O. (1996). *The general method of social work practice* (3rd ed.). Boston: Allyn & Bacon.

Mickelson, J. S. (1995). Advocacy. In *Encyclopedia of social work* (19th ed.). Washington, DC: NASW Press.

Milbrath, L. (1965). *Political participation.* Chicago: Rand McNally.

Mills, H. (2000). *Artful persuasion: The new psychology of influence.* New York: AMACOM.

Mosteller, F. (1977). Assessing unknown numbers: Order of magnitude estimation. In W. Fairley & F. Mosteller (Eds.), *Statistics and public policy* (pp. 163-164). Reading, MA: Addison-Wesley.

Nagel, S. (2002). *Handbook of public policy evaluation.* Thousand Oaks, CA: Sage.

National Association of Social Workers. (1995). Political involvement high. *NASW News, 40*(9), 1.

National Association of Social Workers. (1999). *Code of ethics.* Washington, DC: NASW Press.

Nie, N., & Verba, S. (1975). Political participation. In F. Greenstein & N. Polsby (Eds.), *Handbook of Political Science* (Vol. 4, pp. 1–98). Reading, MA: Addison-Wesley.

Nozick, R. (1974). *Anarchy, state and utopia.* New York: Basic Books.

Osborn, A. (1963). *Applied imagination* (3rd ed.). New York: Scribner.

Patton, C., & Sawicki, D. (1993). *Basic methods of policy analysis and planning* (2nd ed.). Englewood Cliffs, NJ: Prentice Hall.

Pawlak, E., & Flynn, J. (1990). Executive directors' political activities. *Social Work, 35*(4), 307–312.

Perlman, H. (1957). *Casework: A problem solving process.* Chicago: University of Chicago Press.

Perloff, R. (1993). *The dynamics of persuasion.* Hillsdale, NJ: Lawrence Erlbaum Associates, Publishers.

Rainie, L., Cornfield, M., & Horrigan, J. (2005). *The internet and campaign 2004.* Washington, DC: The Pew Research Center for the People and the Press.

Rawls, J. (1971). *A theory of justice.* Cambridge, MA: Harvard University Press.

Reamer, F. (1993). *The philosophical foundations of social work.* New York: Columbia University Press.

Reeser, L., & Epstein, I. (1987). Social workers' attitudes toward poverty and social action: 1968–1984. *Social Service Review, 61*(4), 610–622.

Reingen, P., & Kernan, J. (1993). Social perception and interpersonal influence: Some consequences of the physical attractiveness stereotype in a personal selling setting. *Journal of Consumer Psychology, 2*(1), 25–38.

Reisch, M. (1995). If you think you're not political, guess again. *NASW Network, 21*(13), 1, 10.

Rhoads, K. (1997). What's in a frame? In *Working Psychology.* Retrieved June 27, 2004, from www.workingpsychology.com/whatfram.html

Rhoads, K., & Cialdini, R. (2002). The business of influence: Principles that lead to success in commercial settings. In J. Dillard & M. Pfau (Eds.), *The persuasion handbook* (pp. 513–542). Thousand Oaks, CA: Sage.

Richan, W. (1996). *Lobbying for social change* (2nd ed.). New York: Haworth Press.

Roberts, A., & Yeager, K. (Eds.). (2004). *Evidence based practice manual: Research and outcome measures in health and human services.* New York: Oxford University Press.

Roberts, H., III, Evans, H., Honeman, D., & Balch, T. (2000). *Robert's Rules of Order* (10th ed.). New York: HarperCollins.

Rosenthal, A. (1993). *The third house: Lobbyists and lobbying in the states.* Washington, DC: CQ Press.

Rossi, P., Lipsey, M., & Freeman, H. (2004). *Evaluation: A systematic approach* (7th ed.). Thousand Oaks, CA: Sage.

Royce, D., Thyer, B., Padgett, D., & Logan, T. (2006). *Program evaluation: An introduction* (4th ed.). Belmont, CA: Thomson.

Salcido, R. M. (1984). Social work practice in political campaigns. *Social Work, 29*(2), 189–191.

SASSI Institute. (n.d.). *Welcome to the SASSI web site.* Retrieved September 6, 2004, from www.sassi.com/saddi/index.shtml

Schein, E. H. (1997). *Organizational culture and leadership* (2nd ed.). San Francisco: Jossey-Bass.

Schiller, B. (2004). *The economics of poverty and discrimination* (9th ed.). Upper Saddle River, NJ: Prentice-Hall.

Schneider, R., & Lester, L. (2001). *Social work advocacy: A new framework for action.* Belmont, CA: Brooks/Cole.

Shavelson, R., McDonnell, L., & Oakes, J. (1991). What are educational indicators and indicator systems? *Practical Assessment, Research & Evaluation, 2*(11). Retrieved September 6, 2004, from http://PAREonline.net/getvn.asp?v=2&n=11

Stanley, H., & Niemi, R. (1995). *Vital statistics on American politics* (5th ed.). Washington, DC: Congressional Quarterly Press.

Sunley, R. (1997). Advocacy in the new world of managed care. *Families in Society, 78*(1), 84–94.

Van Soest, D. (1995). Peace and social justice. In R. Edwards (Ed.), *Encyclopedia of social work* (19th ed., pp. 1810–1817). Washington, DC: NASW Press.

Verba, S., Schlozman, K., & Brady, H. (1995). *Voice and equality.* Cambridge, MA: Harvard University Press.

Webster M., Jr., & Driskell, J., Jr. (1983). Beauty as status. *American Journal of Sociology, 89*, 140–165.

Wilson, W. (1887). The study of administration. *Political Science Quarterly, 2*(2), 197–222.

W. K. Kellogg Foundation. (2004). *Logic model development guide.* Battle Creek, MI: W. K. Kellogg Foundation.

Wolk, J. L. (1981). Are social workers politically active? *Social Work, 26*(4), 283–288.

Wolk, J., Pray, E., Weismiller, T., & Dempsey, D. (1996). Political practica: Educating social work students for policymaking. *Journal of Social Work Education, 32*(1), 91–100.

Wolpe, B., & Levine, B. (1996). *Lobbying Congress: How the system works.* Washington, DC: Congressional Quarterly Press.

INDEX